TITANIC
THE TENNIS STORY

LINDSAY GIBBS

Titanic: The Tennis Story is published by New Chapter Press (www.NewChapterMedia.com) and distributed by the Independent Publishers Group (www.IPGBook.com). Randy Walker is the Publisher/Managing Partner for New Chapter Press. Follow this book on FACEBOOK at "Titanic: The Tennis Story" fan page.

The front and back cover of the book was designed by Sumit Srivastava.

The interior was designed by Peggy Swanson.

The front cover photo is courtesy of Corbis.

ISBN – 978-1-937559-04-5

Printed in the United States of America.

Contents

1

The locker room at the Newport Casino was silent. Dick hated silence.

This had not always been the case. He used to love the quiet, he used to seek it out, crave it. His favorite moments growing up had been when he found time to himself in the Swiss countryside, just watching the world and enjoying the silence. A chance to think.

But now silence was his worst enemy. Now when things were silent his mind filled the void with echoes of cries. Without diversion, his mind had a harder time warding off the detailed memories of the ship. The archways, the marble staircase, the carvings in the wood.

In the last couple of years, he had become an expert at small talk. He had mastered his father's act of talking to strangers. Once the shy athletic star, he now had in-depth conversations about the weather, fashion, politics. He would start a conversation about anything, with absolutely anyone. Because when things were this silent, this still, he felt the ground moving underneath him, as though rocking on a wave. He saw the smokestack falling. He felt the water.

A locker slamming aggressively shut came as a welcome distraction. The horror disappeared and his head instinctively turned in the direction of the sound. There he was, in the greatest of ironies. Karl Behr. The only person in the world he didn't dare engage in small talk with. The only person in the world who didn't provide a distraction from the thoughts.

The only person who made it worse. Unfortunately, he was the only other person in the locker room right now. They were about to face off in the quarterfinals of the lawn tennis championships of the United States.

He quickly jerked his head back around and resumed tying his shoes. Had Karl been looking at him? Did he seem angry? Did he look like he was about to speak? What if he tried to talk first? What if Helen came by to wish him luck? He wished tying his shoes was a more complicated activity so he could shut out these thoughts. He had promised himself he wasn't going to do this. He had promised himself that this was just another match. He would not fall apart now, not when he had come so far.

Sweat poured down his face and he was unsure whether it was the Rhode Island late August heat, the stuffiness of the musty locker room this late in the tournament, or his over-active nerves that was causing such a reaction. He was sure that this was not the way to be feeling right before such a big match, no matter who the opponent was. *He had to get himself together.*

This was the quarterfinals of the U.S. Nationals, for God's sake. This was his year. Two years ago he'd taken Maurice McLoughlin to five sets, and last year he'd lost to Mac again, but in the final. Now he was the defending finalist and this was the year he was finally going to do it. He was going to lift that trophy he had been hearing about since he was a youngster. He'd held so many tennis trophies; would this one feel different? He wouldn't ever find out if he didn't get himself together here. He checked the tension of his racket strings. It was of course just perfect. He always made sure it was perfect. Tight, but not "board tight."

The only thing that mattered was winning this match. Win this match. Win two more. Win the trophy. That was it. Simple. He had the talent. He had the shots, the fitness, the desire...He had it all. He just had to stay focused and to not let anything or anyone get in the way.

The door opened and a portly tournament official broke the silence with his expected announcement: "Mr. Behr, Mr. Williams, it is time to take the court."

Neither man said a word. Dick still didn't look up, unwilling to risk a moment of conversation until a net was between them. He sensed Karl picking up his racket bag and when he heard the footsteps pass him, he followed, looking down at his shoes the whole time. He felt again for his rackets and towels to make sure everything was in place. He took a deep breath and jumped up and down a bit as he walked to get his blood flowing. Jumped up and down on healthy legs. His healthy legs that he wouldn't have if it wasn't for...

The chatter, and then cheers, of the Newport crowd came just in time to stop the train of thought.

Just another opponent.

Just win this one match.

Just don't think.

2

"Another one, Mr. Behr?"

Karl nodded at the elderly bartender without looking up, a skill he had mastered these past few weeks. He was frightened that if he looked up he would accidentally catch a reflection of himself. The tall and formerly dashing gentleman was afraid that his outsides were beginning to match his insides and that was not a reality he was quite yet ready to face.

It had been twenty-five days since he had last seen or heard from her. *Twenty-five days.*

Momentary relief came when a second glass of scotch appeared in front of him. He'd have to savor that one. He only allowed himself three per night, an arbitrary limit he had put in place to preserve his rapidly fading dignity. He would be completely ashamed if his family and friends back in Brooklyn saw him in this state, especially his three older brothers who were always giving him a hard time about his melodramatic sensibilities.

Supposedly, he was in Vienna on business. His days were busy conducting meetings for his father's successful adhesives company, Herman Behr & Co., but the evenings were pure anguish. All he could do was wait. This nameless, candle-lit bar buried around the corner from his hotel provided him a little bit of comfort though. Every evening, for twenty-four evenings now, he sat with an eclectic mixture of haves and have nots, all bound together by a common desire to escape.

Of course this bar was just like every other bar. The troubled patrons came in to forget their problems, but after a drink – or four – their problems were...all they talked about. Everyone had a story. Karl was no different.

His tale was as romantic as it was foolish. Six weeks ago he left behind his successful life as a tennis player and lawyer in New York to chase after a girl. Helen Newsom was the love of his life. They were meant to be together, he was certain of that. Or at least he *had* been certain.

He had been seeing Helen for over a year now. His younger sister Gertie had set them up last February and they had been inseparable ever since. He was passionate and charismatic. She was feisty and fun-loving. Together they made the perfect pair. There was only one problem – she was nineteen and he was twenty-seven and her mother did not approve. At all.

In an effort to cool down their rapidly escalating relationship (and, Karl was convinced, to find new "appropriate" suitors) Helen's mother, Sallie Beckwith, had arranged to take her away on a trip across Europe. Horrified at the thought of spending so much time away from one another, and feeling as though time was running out to win Mrs. Beckwith's approval, he and Helen had devised a plan. He would take some time off at the law firm and take a job in Europe for his father – after first joining her family for ten days of their trip.

They had a romantic and unforgettable week and a half together, turning Portugal, Algeria, the south of France and everywhere in between, into their own romantic playground. But Mrs. Beckwith had not budged. If anything she had grown more hostile towards him as the trip went on. The more charming and helpful he was, the more unwelcoming she was in return. The tension started to wear heavily on

Helen. By the time they went their separate ways in Nice, the situation was so uncomfortable that he couldn't help but wonder if Helen had finally had enough, if she was finally ready to listen to her mother and lead a simpler life with a hand-chosen pedigree suitor. He knew Helen loved him, but was that enough?

He provided her with his address in Vienna and the plan was for her to write him when she and her family were headed back to America, instructing him where to meet. He promised he would wait for her. But after twenty-five days without a word, it was beginning to feel hopeless. He was starting to fear the absolute worst.

His second scotch was getting low. Karl sighed as his only joy of the day began to slip away. He fiddled in his pocket with a ring – his mother's ring – that he brought to Europe with the intent of proposing to Helen once he received approval from her parents. He still carried it with him everywhere. He cursed himself inwardly for not fighting harder for her, for being so stubborn and respectful that he had to wait for her parent's permission. Why was he so damned polite?

He took a deep breath, letting the heavy smoke in the bar settle deep into his lungs. He ran his fingers through his long and messy blonde hair and his hands rested on his unshaven face. He couldn't remember the last time he had been to the barber. How had he let himself get like this?

"Pardon, Mr. Behr?" A meek female voice asked, tapping him on the shoulder.

"Yes," he said, startled. "Can I help you?"

His eyes, which had been transfixed on a glass of scotch, turned towards the young front-desk receptionist from his hotel standing next to him holding a telegram.

"Excuse me for interrupting you, Mr. Behr, but I have a telegram for you."

```
DEAREST KARL STOP HAVE PROCURED
FIRST CLASS TICKETS ON TITANIC
STOP LEAVING NEXT WEEK STOP
PLEASE JOIN US STOP LOVE HELEN
```

He did not think his heart had ever beat this fast. Not in the 1907 doubles final at Wimbledon, the grandest tennis tournament in the world, when he and Beals Wright took on the storied and accomplished Australasian doubles team of Norman Brookes and Tony Wilding. Not in the semifinals of the "all-comers" tournament at the 1906 U.S. Nationals when he was down two sets to one to Raymond Little and had to save seven match points before winning in five sets. Not even the first time he saw Helen. This was without a doubt the most anxious he had ever been.

The next few days were a whirlwind. Though the *Titanic* was surprisingly not fully booked, it still ended up being a bit of an aggravation – and an expense – to secure a first-class ticket. He had to quickly wrap up his business loose ends, which was harder to do on the turn of a dime than he had expected. He sent a telegram home to tell his family to anticipate his arrival and went to the barber to get himself cleaned up. While in Paris, he stopped to pick up a couple of gifts for Helen's parents that he trusted would help to finally break the ice.

On the *Transatlantique* train to the port of Cherbourg, he finally had a chance to unwind a bit, his heart beating in almost synchronicity with the clang of the railroad cars. Perhaps his heart beat was just his body's way of drowning out the chaos of the train or that he was just so excited to be moving and functioning after he had let himself so dramatically slip into the depths of despair the past few weeks over what seemed now to be nothing. Or perhaps his heart was right to beat that hard. After all, the confrontation to come with Helen's mother was enough to give even Mac McLoughlin a shaky racket hand. All he knew was that he was not going to budge. He stood braced against a wall at the front of a car, his singular trunk sitting on his seat nearby where he could keep an eye on it. It seemed paranoid, especially in the throws of first-class travel, but his father had always beat into his head to never let his luggage out of his sight. It was a rare lesson that had actually stuck.

Gertie had sent him a telegram before he left Vienna. "Slow, steady and careful," it read, echoing advice that their mother had given all the children when they were growing up. "Be safe Karly." His little sister, while supportive of the relationship between her older brother and best friend, was very much the voice of reason. She knew that they were both impulsive and that without anyone to slow them down things could escalate quickly.

There were six Behr children, four boys (Max, Frederich, Herman, Jr., and Karl) and two girls (Gertrude and Margaret). Karl was the youngest of the boys and Gertie the youngest of all, and the two had always had a special bond as many younger siblings do, trying to navigate their own place in an already established and thriving family.

Gertie, always the shy and practical one of the family, really came into her own when she went away to school at Briarcliff Manor in New York. Seemingly overnight, she transformed into a passionate, motivated and independent woman. She attended women's meetings and began to become interested in what was being called the "women's rights movement." It was exciting to see his little sister find a voice of her own and even more exciting to see her ruffle the feathers of their conservative family a bit by doing so. He could see so much of their mother in Gertie, or at least the person their mother had wanted to be.

Grace Behr passed away in 1907. All of the Behr children were, in their own ways, still reeling from the death of their mother. Karl's older sister Margaret barely saw the family since. Frederich rushed into an obviously doomed marriage. Max lost himself in the sport of golf. Herman went into a deep depression that only ceased when his wife had their first child. Karl did his best to keep himself together and become the type of man his mother would have wanted him to be – loyal, hardworking and passionate. But the loss had hit Gertie the hardest. She had spent the most time around their mother while she was sick. As the youngest, she was the one who had still needed her the most. It wasn't until she went to Briarcliff that it seemed she began to heal.

The previous February, Gertie brought her best college friend, Helen Newsom, home to Brooklyn to plan out their activities at school for the following year. They were getting a group of women together to join the women's suffrage movement in New York, so they could help arrange rallies and awareness. Strangely enough, they decided to meet outside in the yard despite the cold weather, probably so that they wouldn't be bothered by any of the many boys going in and out of the house.

When Karl first laid eyes on Helen he was entranced. He peered through the kitchen window and saw Gertie and Helen in the backyard sitting on the bench their father had built underneath the now bare oak tree, both bundled in coats and scarves. The snow was coming down but they didn't seem to notice. Helen was gorgeous but not in the way that most girls he had dated were. She wasn't trying to flaunt her beauty at all. She sat up straight, her shoulders back, but it wasn't in an awkward or pretentious way; rather it seemed to be just the natural way for her to hold herself.

He had rarely felt even the smallest hint of nerves. In fact, he was famous for his sang-froid on the tennis court. But he could feel the jitters brewing inside him now, and rather than succumb to such things, he grabbed his jacket and boots and dashed outside. He didn't have the faintest idea what he would say to her but he knew he had to meet her. He needed to hear her voice and look into her eyes. He needed to see if he was going crazy. This was no time to play it safe from the baseline.

As he walked out she looked over at him. They locked eyes and his entire body went numb. He had never believed in love at first sight before, but he proved to be a quick convert. She smiled at him and didn't look away. Could she possibly be feeling it too? Could he be so lucky?

"Helen, I'd like you to meet my brother," Gertie said.

"Karl Behr, the star tennis player, right? Gertie's told me a lot about you," Helen said.

Her voice was divine. Raspy, warm, sincere. He was in trouble.

"Oh, don't believe a thing she tells you. I am delighted to meet you Helen." His voice, on the other hand, was shaky and squawky. He sounded like a thirteen-year-old. He stuck out his hand to shake hers, only for an excuse to touch, even through her mittens. They went in for lunch, after which he invited her to go on a walk with him. She said yes. They had been together ever since.

Their courtship progressed rapidly, but it all seemed very natural. They both had busy schedules, with Helen leading every activity possible at Briarcliff and Karl's tennis career and involvement in his father's business expanding. But written correspondence, the occasional phone call and visits whenever possible advanced the romance quickly. There wasn't a doubt in Karl's mind from early on that he and Helen were to get married.

Everything changed when Helen's mother sensed the intensity of their relationship. She happened upon a stack of letters from Karl when she was visiting Helen at Briarcliff that winter and nearly had a breakdown. She moved Helen out of school and back to live with her and began screening her letters and correspondence. When she realized they were still managing to communicate despite her best efforts, she took Helen off to Europe.

But he was not going to go away that easily. He might have let Mrs. Beckwith get the best of him during their ten days together in Europe, but now the game was different. They would be trapped on a ship together, surrounded by others whom he could win over first, like early-round opponents on the tennis courts at Newport. He was not going to get off of that ship without winning over Sallie and Richard Beckwith and proposing to Helen. He searched his coat pocket for the ring, checking that it was there for about the twentieth time that day. He looked around the hectic train and noticed the families all around him. Mothers, children, fathers. He hoped that this would be his last journey ever as a single man.

3

Honk Honk!

Sitting in the cramped backseat of a Renault taxi, Dick Williams was having a hard time controlling his laughter. The car raced through the streets of Paris, dodging tourists and businessmen, cars and horses as it tried to keep pace with the identical and even more headlong-driven car right in front of them. On this early morning of April 10, 1912 Dick and his father Charles Duane Williams, riding in the car in front, were running very late.

> *Anyone who knows me could not suppose me*
> *Gloomy, or glum, or sad!*
> *Generally times are bad*
> *I am always gay and glad!*

A song from the opera his father had taken him to the previous night, *The Count of Luxembourg*, was stuck in his head and he found himself humming it out loud. The driver was giving him a perturbed look, but that only encouraged him. He checked his pocket watch and realized just how close they were cutting it – their train to Cherbourg, the port where they were to catch their ship, was scheduled to depart in just ten minutes. He still couldn't bring himself to worry though – things like this always worked out. Of course his father, in the other taxi, would be in an entirely different mood.

The morning started off smoothly enough. Dick and his father had packed their trunks in their Paris hotel room, loaded them into matching taxis and headed off to the train station. Unfortunately, they had headed to the wrong train station. When his car pulled up, his father was standing outside the station flailing his arms about wildly, ordering the cabs to the other side of town. The image of his composed, dignified father flapping about like a bird had Dick in stitches.

His father had reason to be nervous of course. They were moving to America but were in great danger of missing their ship. Though they were American citizens, they had lived in Geneva, where Dick was born. Their family had settled in Switzerland due to his father's delicate health. The fresh mountain air was supposed to revive him, but Dick suspected that wasn't why they'd stayed. The endless blue sky, crystal clear lakes and picturesque mountains were certainly a luxurious environment for anyone. But more so than that, it was the people, and the minor celebrity status that they had been able to attain, that he thought had kept them in Switzerland for so long.

However, it was all about to change. They were headed back to America where they would reside with Charles's brother (and Dick's namesake) Richard Norris Williams in Pennsylvania for the summer until Dick went off to Harvard in the fall. Oh, and he was supposed to play tennis. *Lots and lots of tennis.* That was, of course, if they made their boat!

They booked passage on board what was supposed to be the finest ship ever made, the White Star Line's RMS *Titanic*. Dick became fascinated reading about this ship in the papers when he came down with a bad case of the measles earlier that year. When the illness caused them to have to postpone their original trip in February, he lobbied his father hard to book tickets on *Titanic*.

It didn't take much convincing, for being on the maiden voyage of such a grand ship would be a story to tell for a lifetime. The April departure was a bit later than Charles had hoped for, but Dick was sure that his father was thrilled with the decision. It was an honor to be a part of the debut of such a ship – some of the most prominent members of society would be on board, including millionaire John Jacob Astor IV and his wife, industrialist Benjamin Guggenheim, Macy's owner Isidor Straus and Denver millionairess Margaret "Molly" Brown. He would be inconsolable if they missed the ship now, but Dick wasn't too concerned. The Gare St. Lazare train station was in sight. He checked his pocket watch – five minutes to spare.

The taxi screeched to a halt and Dick threw some money at his driver while his frantic father colorfully instructed the porters with the trolley cart where to take the luggage. The two men then went dashing through the station to make their train.

He loved the Gare St. Lazare. It was one of the most beautiful buildings in Paris. It's arched, vaulted ceilings had windows at the top and the way the light streamed through at certain times of the day made the entire station glow. When he had time to spare during his frequent travels, Dick loved to sit on a bench and watch the hurried travelers race by. Of course, there was no time to sit and observe today. They raced through the station, pushing bystanders out of the way and making quite a scene.

"One minute! We have one minute Richard Norris, hurry up!" Charles yelled from up ahead.

He *hated* when his father called him by his full name. He also hated the fact that his frail, fifty-one-year-old father was running faster than him.

14

As the train departure whistle blew, Dick went into a final kick, passed his father and made it to the train. He held the door as Charles limped up the stairs, completely out of breath. The doors closed immediately behind them. The whistle blew again and the train was off.

As soon as they got settled into their seats – in the back of the first-class car, on the right side, just like Charles always preferred – the moleskin notebook came out. As long as Dick could remember, his father carried around a moleskin note-book. He wrote nothing in them about the law, or finances, or even family. The moleskins were devoted to Charles's number one passion in life – tennis. He had stacks of them, chronicling everything from the very first tennis match he had ever seen, to the playing patterns and styles of some of the most notable players in the world, to the plans he had to develop an international governing body for the sport.

Today the moleskin was fresh. New journey, new note-book. He peered over his father's shoulder to observe the ritual. Charles bent the notebook to break it in faster, flipped through the pages, made a crease so it sat flat on the tabletop, and carefully wrote in the heading, "Road to the winning the U.S. National Singles Title." He looked up at Dick with a huge grin on his face.

"All right, Richard Norris, let's get started," Charles said, not even bothering to contain his excitement.

The U.S. Nationals at Newport was the biggest tennis tour-nament in the United States. It was the national championship of the United States, started in 1881 by the newly-organized U.S. National Lawn Tennis Association. The lush green lawns of the courts at the Newport Casino – and the stories of the legendary players and great matches that were contested on them – was what significantly stoked Charles's love of the sport.

As a child, Dick's bedtime stories had been about famous tennis matches, the heroes the great players of the sport's early decades – after all, lawn tennis had only been formally organized by Major Walter Clopton Wingfield in Britain in 1874. Dick started playing when he was five in 1896. By the time he was seven, his father was teaching him strokes and tactics. At nine, he began playing against much older players at the Avantes Lawn and Tennis Club outside Geneva. He was soon winning all the local tournaments for boys in Switzerland. In his late teens, he began traveling to other tournaments in Europe, rarely losing. He really loved tennis. He was a shy and awkward boy and the tennis court was one of the few places he felt comfortable. And like most young boys, he just wanted to please his father.

But he was no longer a boy and the rising expectations he faced as a tournament player made him uncomfortable. It began to feel like pressure. *A lot of pressure.* The game had come to define him and he wanted to explore who he was outside of a tennis court. He wanted to make friends with people who weren't competitors and to figure out his own interests. He wanted to be his own person and find his own identity. He loved to play tennis, but he was not sure he shared the same passion for the sport that his father had. He was hoping that this move to America would be a time for him to start fresh.

The only problem was, he hadn't been able to summon the courage to talk about his feelings to his father. In fact, he hadn't talked to anyone about it. All of his friends in Geneva were tennis friends, his father's friends, or his father's tennis friends. He was so entwined in it all that he didn't know if there actually was a way out. His father was excited at the talents of his young boy and he had big expectations, like any proud parent would have.

"I'm really hungry, Pops, I'm going to go to the dining car first," he said, trying not to sound too exasperated.

"All right, son," Charles replied, already scribbling away in the moleskin.

The first-class car on the *Transatlantique* was full of passengers heading to Cherbourg to board the *Titanic*. Some of the most powerful men in America and Europe, who were booked on the ship, were likely on the train. Society and social standing were foreign concepts to Dick. Perhaps it was because he grew up in Switzerland, or because he had parents who didn't feel the need to display their wealth ostentatiously, but he just did not understand what the big deal was. Women's fashion especially confused him.

For instance, even now while traveling six hours on a train ride that they must have known would be cramped and uncomfortable no matter how expensive the tickets, the women were dressed head to toe in the most lavish and uncomfortable looking garments he'd ever seen. Tight dresses that threatened to squeeze the breath out of them with skirts that were either so tight or so massive that it was impossible to walk like a dignified human being – even though they were dressing that way just so they'd be perceived as such. And forget about the hats! It seemed to Dick as if they should have booked an entire extra train car just for the hats.

And this was just the train ride. He tried to picture what the *Titanic* would look like – the dining room, the smoking room, the gymnasium. He hoped it was as good as the brochures and articles made it seem. He hoped the ship had a lot of space, endless corridors for exploring. He wondered what color the walls of his room would be and whether the stewards and stewardesses would be wearing the same uniforms as on his last ship ride. He was ten years old at the time and for some reason he had found the uniforms to be just the most fascinating things – they always looked so cleanly pressed!

Walking through the train, he had to dodge children, stray luggage and stewards alike. He felt like that morning's taxi driver slaloming through the Paris traffic. As he crossed through to another car a man at the other end caught his eye. In the midst of the chaos he was standing perfectly still, propped up against the side of the car and gazing out the window. He looked deep in thought, as if he had found a secret way to drown out all of the bustle around him.

As Dick walked closer he began to realize that this man looked familiar – yes, he knew this man! It was Karl Behr, the great tennis champion from the United States. He could hardly believe it. Behr had been ranked in the top ten for several years and Dick's father had often tried to get him to emulate Behr's drive volley, which was one of the best in the game. Dick followed Karl's career and was well aware of his exploits reaching the Wimbledon doubles final in 1907 and also being a member of the challenging U.S. Davis Cup team that year. Dick admired the stories he read of Behr's aggressive and athletic play and regarded him as a paragon of athleticism and fitness as the winner of many extended five-set matches.

He wanted to go run and tell his father, but Charles would surely hound the tennis star for the remainder of the trip, so he decided against it. Behr looked to be enjoying his quiet and solitude. It was strange though – here Dick wanted a short respite from his father's tennis talk and he ended up running into a famous tennis player. Dick laughed at the irony.

4

After disembarking the *Transatlantique* at Cherbourg, the *Titanic* passengers faced an unplanned delay. When the *Titanic* embarked on its maiden voyage from Southampton, England that morning she had a near collision with another liner, *SS New York*, that caused an hour's delay. The 142 first-class passengers, 30 second-class passengers and 102 third-class passengers all waited impatiently for the gigantic new liner to make it across the English Channel. Finally, around 5:30 p.m., they were loaded onto two tenders – the *Nomadic* for first and second-class passengers and the *Traffic* for third-class – and taken out to sea to board the great ship. The Port of Cherbourg was just too shallow for a ship the size of the *Titanic* to pull into the dock.

On board the *Nomadic,* Dick and his father waited anxiously with other passengers on the decks, hoping to be the first person to get a glimpse of the famous ship. Dick couldn't stop laughing because anytime any boat was spotted in the ocean everyone aboard would go running and crowd the deck to spot it, when most of the time it was just another tender, private boat or steamship. It happened so often that it seemed like some were doing it purely to amuse themselves. At dusk, the *Titanic* finally came into view and there was no mistaking it. A hush came over the crowd.

Dick had read all of the statistics – the *Titanic* was 882 feet long, 92 feet wide, 175 feet tall, had four giant smokestacks, 16 watertight compartments and weighed 46,000 tons. As the

Nomadic pulled to the starboard side of the anchored ship and the gangway was lowered, he looked over at his father and realized that they were wearing matching grins. This was not just a ship, it was a city. The band played the *Marseilles* as the breathless passengers carefully climbed the gangway into the hallows of the ship's E Deck. This was definitely worth the wait.

Dick gave their names to a stewardess and got directions to their cabin. He was giddy with excitement, a feeling he hadn't felt in quite some time. There was so much to see, so much free space to roam, so many distractions – this was exactly what he needed, a chance to clear his mind.

Their stateroom, D-14, was located on the starboard side of the ship in an enviable location, right next to the Grand Staircase and dining room. It was beautiful, even by the standards of the posh European hotels that Charles and Dick were used to. There was a queen-size bed on each side of the door. At the end of the room, there was an L-shaped nook where a porthole was located. The walls were white with Edwardian-style molding and the room was decorated in gold and red accents. There was a vanity, a closet and a small chair to sit in.

Somehow a stewardess was already unpacking their things when they got there, but Charles, ever the busybody, was redoing everything immediately after her. Dick was anxious to go to the upper decks and start looking around.

"Come on Pops, let's go up to the deck and wave goodbye to Cherbourg!"

Charles looked at him like he was crazy. He grabbed their tuxedos from the closet and handed his to him. "There's plenty of time to do that tomorrow. Right now we are late for our dinner plans."

—❦❦❦—

Everything was a blur to Karl. The exit from the train, the wait for the ship, the ride on the *Nomadic*, the boarding. The anticipation of finding Helen had turned him into a maelstrom of nerves and uncertainty. Somewhere in the travels of the day it had occurred to him that he didn't have the slightest semblance of a plan.

Everything happened so quickly after he received the telegram that his entire focus had been on getting to the ship, and not on what he was going to do once he was there! *How* exactly was he going to win Sallie and Richard Beckwith over? How was he going to propose?

To top it off, this ship was too big for its own good. Despite several stewardesses pointing him in the right direction, he could not manage to find his stateroom! What in the world would anyone need all of this space for? Of course, if he had been able to step outside of himself for a moment he would have seen that he was on board the ship of dreams and that he was one of the luckiest men in the world. His first-class ticket – purchased on a whim – delineated him as one of the select few members of society privileged enough to experience this remarkable achievement of modern technology. But Karl was physically and emotionally unable to see things as they were. This historic nautical achievement of man was nothing more than the staging ground for his own personal quest. And the record size of the ship merely represented one more obstacle in finding Helen.

After endless twists and turns down identical corridors he finally found his room, Cabin C-148. It was a fine room, comparable to the nicest hotel room he had stayed in, but he didn't take time to notice any of the details. His luggage wasn't there yet! How was that possible? One would have assumed, considering how long it took him to find his room, that the staff of this incomparable ship could have managed to have his luggage beat him there. Apparently, that was not the case. His father was right: it was increasingly difficult to get good service these days.

A quick glimpse into the mirror had him completely appalled. He looked just about as confident and presentable as he felt. And without his suitcase, he couldn't even improve the latter condition. He couldn't let anyone, especially Helen, see him like this. He thought about waiting, but patience had never been his virtue, whether on the tennis court, in business or in love. Helen was on this ship and he could not wait another second to go find her. It might be foolish to risk Mrs. Beckwith seeing him in this state, but nothing could stop him. It had been *thirty days*. He straightened his collar, smoothed out his hair a bit, rubbed the ring in his pocket for good luck and bolted out the door.

At the end of the hallway there was a tall, slender, young brunette stewardess, dressed in white from head to toe. She looked remarkably like Helen, and had she not been in uniform, in his crazed state he might have confused the two. But nonetheless he considered it a good sign. In any case, he felt somehow comforted by the resemblance.

"Excuse me Miss…"

"Newsom. How can I help you sir?"

He did a double-take upon hearing Helen's last name, but luckily he focused in on her name tag before getting carried away – her surname was in fact Newton, and he was in fact going crazy. Still, he felt again it was some sort of omen.

"Yes, Miss Newton. I was wondering if you might help me locate a Miss Helen Newsom." Even as he over-articulated the final syllable, he felt it must surely make him sound as deranged as he felt.

"Well, sir, we haven't yet released the first-class passenger list, and it's not polite for me to give out a lady's room number, even to such a handsome man as yourself. Who knows what your intentions are?"

On other, earlier, sea crossings he would have welcomed – even encouraged – a good innocent flirtation, but the only welcome aspect of this one was the comfort of knowing that he must not look quite as haggard as he felt.

"Well, I can tell you what my intentions are."

He flashed his most charming smile and brought the ring out of his coat pocket.

Miss Newton fairly melted at the sight. Women and rings, it was a foolproof equation. But would it work on the two most stubborn women in the world — Sallie Beckwith and Helen Newsom?

"You see Miss Newton, I intend to ask Helen to be my wife. Do you think I can get her room number?"

The stewardess went behind a door in the corner and pulled out a directory. "Room C-35. Good luck!" She shouted after him.

He walked briskly through the corridors, now suddenly feeling like a master navigator. He found her room and knocked, but there was no answer. He was getting frustrated and impatient. If he were this easily discouraged on the tennis court, he'd have never made all those comebacks from one or two sets down. What had the papers said after his miraculous comeback against Raymond Little?

"One of the most remarkable exhibitions of grit and nerve under the most crushing grind that has ever been witnessed on the famous courts of Newport."

He'd memorized it and never forgotten it these six years. So think, he told himself. There's always a strategy. Did he stay there and wait for her? That was the easiest solution but of course he risked running into Mrs. Beckwith first, which might make him look more like a pest than a future fiancé. While he was struggling to decide to search or stay, he realized just how hungry he was – in his state of nervousness he had neglected to eat all day – and he decided that there was no better place to start his search than the dining room.

It wasn't until he was standing at the three-tiered Grand Staircase platform on the C Deck, looking down at the lounge that led to the dining room, that he stopped to realize where he was. He was on board the finest ship known to man. In all his travels, in all his success, he had not ever been anywhere quite as grand. It was the epitome of class, sophistication and, most importantly of all, romance. This was the perfect place to propose. This ship was the perfect stage for his and Helen's love to be solidified.

He scanned over the lounge and observed the impeccably dressed upper class of society and their endless parade gowns and glamour. There was no so sign of Helen. He felt frustrated but love had led him this far. Certainly, there was no backing out now.

"Karl!"

His entire body was flushed in a second, overcome with happiness. *It was her voice* and it sounded glad. Suddenly there she was, barreling up the stairs in her high heels, strapped as though in a straitjacket in a dress that was absolutely stunning but that he was sure she loathed. And then she was in his arms, kissing him, making a spectacle.

He was sure that Sallie Beckwith and her friends were watching, but he found for the moment that he didn't care. He didn't even open his eyes. He had done it. They were together again. It was the only thing worth knowing, the only thing worth feeling.

The dining room on the *Titanic* was fit for royalty and most of Dick's fellow passengers expected to be treated as such. There was a blue and gold carpet on the floor. The chairs were plush green. The china was fine and the chandeliers looked as if they'd been dipped in gold. It was all so refined it made him feel like a ruffian in comparison. It was the setting for a grand romance or a scene in the opera.

The company his father kept was just as overwhelming. Their table was filled with some of the richest and most powerful men in America. This included a list of names that Dick had been taught to revere from a young age, including George and Eleanor Widener (rumored to be the wealthiest family in Pennsylvania), Major Archibald Butt (President Taft's Military Aide) and Butt's friend, the famous painter Frank Millet. It would have been intimidating company for anyone.

The most familiar faces in the group were John and Marion Thayer and their seventeen–year-old son Jack. Charles and John had been friends since childhood in Philadelphia. Mr. Thayer was a very rich man, but he was also a very well-respected, hard-working and important man as he was the vice president of the Pennsylvania Railroad. Those adjectives could certainly not be used to describe everyone in the first class. Of course, if you asked Charles about John, these would not be the first things he would bring up. Rather, he'd bring up the fact that John had been a star cricket player.

Dick was always impressed with the way his father mingled with such notables as if there wasn't a doubt in the world that he belonged in such circles. Of course there wasn't. In fact, everyone always seemed to be thrilled that they were in the presence of Charles Duane Williams. Dick sometimes wondered if he were really Charles's son – throughout dinner in this prestigious company he was more interested in counting the crumbs in John Thayer's enormous mustache. These men loved to put the younger ones on the spot with questions of politics and international relations. In these situations, Dick did his best to be invisible.

He was thrilled to sit next to Jack, whom he had gotten to know well through their families' friendship. He first met the Thayers in Philadelphia when he was ten years old and the Thayers had met them in Europe a few times. Jack, for all his family's high connections, was just about as comfortable in social situations as Dick was.

Dick managed to survive the dinner and they all moved to the smoking room. Although it was not typically an activity that he looked forward to, there was something about this particular room that transcended his cynicism. The deep browns and mahoganies were much more comforting than the pinks and crystal of the dining room and the leather sofas were much more comfortable than wicker. There were also stained glass windows that depicted different ports of call where the White Star Line had ships. These images of distant lands led Dick's mind to wander pleasantly during the stuffy conversation – not that he needed any help.

No women were allowed in the smoking room of course. As chauvinistic as it seemed to Dick at first, he realized that there was something very different about even the most proper man when the women were no longer around. It was as if they were all allowed to take a deep breath, relax and speak as they liked. He, too, found himself feeling more relaxed there. The brandy put him at ease in such a situation. His friend Jack was still a virgin to the tastes of alcohol and Dick made sure that he knew what a great thing he was missing out on.

Charles dominated the conversation as he always did, but the great thing about Dick's father was that he was so interested in other people. He would ask just the right question to get a reticent man to come out with his entire life story. Unlike most of the men in there, Charles genuinely wanted to hear it. He had an uncanny knack for reading people and knowing what stories they wanted to tell and what they needed to talk about.

This was a fascinating group, even Dick had to admit. Major Archibald Butt and Francis Millet were of particular interest, perhaps due to their combination of fine pedigree and soft-spoken nature. Both men were so gentle and understated that one would never suspect their worldly accomplishments, a trait that Dick very much admired and found comfort in.

He loved just sitting there, part of such an established group, listening to the stories these men told. They had traveled so many places, met so many dignitaries, loved so many women, made so many mistakes. It seemed as if every one of them could have their lives turned into an opera. Dick often felt like a simpleton in their company. He wondered if his trivial life that revolved around his father and a tennis ball would ever be a story worth telling.

"So, Johnny boy, it looks like you've kept in fairly decent shape. Think you could give the cricket players of today a run for their money?" Charles was even louder than usual, clearly enjoying the conviviality and companionship of the occasion.

"Charles, I think I'm in even better shape than I was when I was twenty, can you believe that?"

Dick hoped that Charles didn't believe that. Nobody should believe that. He slouched deeper in his chair, wishing that he had managed to escape earlier with Jack and go exploring, cursing himself inwardly for having been seduced by the older men's conversation.

"In fact, for example, I'd say I'm in much better shape than your budding tennis star," said John.

"Dick is deceptively strong, my friend," said Charles. "He is in fantastic shape, championship form. You haven't seen him on a tennis court in quite some time."

"How about a challenge?" John exclaimed with a grin.

"I like the way you think," Charles declared.

"A squash match. I'll reserve the court. Me against Richie Norris. I'll look at the schedule in the morning and see when the best time to play will be."

The two men practically had their backs towards the younger of the proposed competitors. Dick slouched down in the couch about as low as he possibly could without sliding off, but he knew it didn't matter in the slightest. He might as well have been out on the deck having a good time.

"John B. Thayer, that is the finest idea you've had in years. From the Williams point of view, that is! You're going to re-gret this one." Charles let out a hearty laugh.

Dick and Jack locked eyes and Jack was having a hard time controlling his laughter. Major Butt looked over at Dick and passed him a glass of brandy, putting his hand on Dick's shoulder.

"Better drink this, son. The game is on!"

Nightfall on the *Titanic* and Karl was in a reverie. He had been on the deck of a boat at night dozens of times, but it had never been like this. He was certain that this was the most beautiful thing he had ever seen. The lights of the ship glistened and were reflected in the water along with the stars in perfect harmony. The orchestra played peaceful waltzes as the passengers, exhausted from such a long day of traveling, began to settle in for the night.

He and Helen leisurely walked the deck of the ship hand in hand, feeling as if they had all the time in the world. Karl held onto Helen's hand tightly with his right hand, while the left fiddled with the ring in his pocket. She looked so regal and stunning. Her dress was olive green with lace accents and the corset top clung magnificently to her figure. He was certain her mother must have picked it and that Helen must hate it. She never enjoyed feeling restricted by anything, most of all clothing.

For a couple of hours they said little, merely soaked in the atmosphere. They stopped to kiss in corridors or lay as two spoons on the giant lounge chairs underneath the stars. They laughed out of sheer joy, often just staring at one another. Karl could hardly believe his luck. Just four days earlier he had been in the depths of despair, certain he had ruined any chance he had with Helen and fearful he might never see her again. Now he was on the grandest ship in the world with the most beautiful girl he had ever seen. It was overwhelming.

But it was getting late and Karl getting a bit anxious. Finding Helen was only part of the plan, the easy part compared to winning over her parents. They couldn't just float in their bubble of bliss forever.

He knew Helen was on the same page as he was when she started playing with her ear. She had beautiful pearls in her ears. When she began to fiddle with them, Karl knew she was about to start talking. It was a sign that he had picked up early in their relationship.

"Karl…"

She sighed and reached out and stroked his face gently and he knew that she wanted him to address the obvious problem now that she had broken the silence. Instead, he reached in to kiss her, but this move didn't go over very well. When Helen was ready to talk she was ready. She pulled away from him, smacking him lightly with her clutch, causing him to erupt with laughter.

"Come on Karl, this is serious. What are we going to do? Do you have a plan?"

"Of course I do!"

Helen took a step back and looked him up and down, a look of doubt covering her whole face.

"Karl Behr, why do I get the feeling that just the opposite is true?"

Karl grinned from ear to ear, pulling her back towards him, breaking through her mood of seriousness. She let out a slight laugh and pecked him on the cheek.

"I do have a plan, actually," he said. "I brought gifts."

"You what?" Helen was having a hard time controlling her laughter and Karl suddenly realized how silly it sounded. He sheepishly held out the bag he'd been carrying around and Helen grabbed it and went rifling through it.

When she got to the broach and carefully unwrapped it, to preserve the packaging, she stopped laughing. She teared up and stood, clutching it to her hands. Karl didn't know how to react. Through all the drama, all the crazy whirlwind of the past seven months, he was not sure he had ever seen Helen shed a tear. Karl wondered if there was something wrong with the gift, or if perhaps she didn't remember when her mother had seen it in the shop.

"It's just like the one in Nice, do you remember?"

Helen nodded, but the tears kept coming. She tried to regain her composure; Karl could see her fighting herself. He got up and went to her, realizing how cold it was and how daintily dressed she was. He draped his coat around her and reached for her shoulder, wanting to do anything to stop the tears, hoping that it was not he who had caused them.

She took the jacket but moved away from his touch.

"Helen, what is it? Did I do something? I don't have to give them the gifts."

Helen chuckled a bit, composing herself. She huddled herself up in his jacket, smelling it, losing herself in it. She turned to face him, still unable to take a step closer in her vulnerable state, as she was not used to anyone seeing her like this.

"I was so afraid you wouldn't come."

Karl affectionately scooped her up in his arms, not allowing her to resist this time. It was all he knew to do. Helen was not an overly emotional woman. She was passionate and full of life and stubborn, but she was so strong. She never showed an air of vulnerability, of neediness, of weakness of any kind. Karl recalled his own anger at the bar in Vienna, how he had begun to doubt her love and commitment to him. He too often got so caught up in his own heartache that he forgot how hard this was on her. She was so close to her mother and had never argued with her about anything until Karl came into her life.

She kissed his cheek and turned away, staring out at the Atlantic Ocean, shivering a bit. "I just don't know how you put up with any of this, Karl. I don't know why you go through all this trouble for me. And when you didn't board at Southampton.... When I didn't see you I mean, I just assumed..."

Karl put his arm back around her.

"It's all right, darling. I'm here now." She put her hand in his and smiled. He once again played with the ring in his pocket, wondering if this was the moment. She had to know how he had planned for this, that he was in this for this rest of his life. But it wasn't the perfect moment yet. He knew that he would be able to do it the right way and he didn't want to sully things now by acting prematurely.

"I better go back now," she said. "Don't want to make things worse by being late."

"Do you want me to go with you?" Karl asked, though the exhaustion from the day was suddenly hitting him like a dose of morphine.

"No, I think I'd better face them now. I'll work on her. The Kimballs are here, which should keep her distracted. Why don't we meet tomorrow when they're in the parlor in the afternoon? Then you can come to dinner with us."

They kissed, passionately, longingly, assuredly. A kiss like that you could wait for.

"I love you Helen."

"I love you too Karl."

The words hung in the air like a promise, a promise that though they were not sleeping in the same bed, that although the world was not perfect and they couldn't be together in this moment, they would be someday soon.

5

Just before noon on April 11, the *Titanic* made its final European stop at Queenstown, Ireland. Dick and Charles stood on the A Deck promenade watching as the ship anchored and the final passengers boarded the ship. They picked up some Irish mail as well – 1,385 stacks to be exact, as the captain later announced – and after a two-hour stop the ship was ready to take on the Atlantic Ocean. Captain Smith blew the whistle and the *Titanic* was off with 2,237 passengers and crew members on board. The next scheduled stop: Pier 60, New York City, in six days.

On the A Deck, right beside the gym, there was a giant map that showed the route the *Titanic* was going to take. Passengers made bets about how far the ship would go each day and tried to predict the exact time they would land in New York. The run mileage would be posted each day at noon. Dick predicted that the ship would go three hundred miles the first day, while his father, ever the optimist, predicted four hundred. Surprisingly, though, they both guessed the exact same landing time – Wednesday, April 18th at 1:30 p.m.

The great thing about traveling by ship, Dick knew, was that in the shortest of times the passengers were brought together into a small, tightly-knit community. The atmosphere would be lively and relaxed. Besides meals, there was virtually no scheduled time. Everyone was more free than at any other time in their lives. Even for the first-class passengers this was a luxury. As Dick stood on the deck of the ship watching the land in the distance grow smaller and smaller, eventually disappearing, his excitement for a new life in the United States grew stronger and stronger.

After lunch, he met up with Jack Thayer and the Widener's twenty-seven-year-old son Harry at the Veranda Palm Court, the light and airy café with locations on both the port and starboard sides of the ship, something he didn't realize until he waited for them on the wrong side for ten minutes. The café had casual wicker furniture, ivy growing up the walls and giant windows through which you could observe everything happening on the A Deck. The boys were planning to play a game of bridge – a game that he was positively awful at. He didn't know anything about Harry other than his last name, but that in fact told him quite a lot. The Wideners were one of the richest families in Pennsylvania. Mr. Widener was born into money and now owned the bank that funded the White Star Line. Knowing this, Dick braced himself for Harry to be of the arrogant variety. He was taken aback when he finally walked into the right Palm Court and the young man sitting with Jack, a short and skinny fellow with slicked back brown hair, a faded suit and a firm handshake, leaped up to greet him.

"Dick Williams! There you are! So good to finally meet you. I'm Harry Widener."

"Nice to meet you too," Dick said, trying to put on a smile. "Widener. That sounds familiar," he joked.

"Don't believe the pomp." Harry smiled and sat down. "I hear you're going to be treating us to a marquee squash match in a few days."

"I'd almost managed to forget about that. I was hoping

Mr. Thayer wouldn't remember any of that this morning."

In fact, his father had managed to not mention it all morning!

"No such luck," said Jack with a grin. "Father has already been down there practicing this morning."

"And my father could not be more excited himself," said Harry in a loud, enthusiastic voice. "He talked about it all morning."

"Really? Is it that big of a deal?"

"We're on a ship, Dick. There's not much else to talk about. You're not excited?" Dick didn't know how to answer that question so he just let it be. He chuckled, which was his default reaction.

"I'd rather just play cards, Harry," he said. "What are we playing?"

"Let's play poker. I'll bet you my muffin," young Jack exclaimed, causing them all to burst out into laughter. Dick felt immensely lucky that he had been able to find others on the ship who were more interested in poker and muffins than cigars and fine china.

"Hey Dick," said Jack. "You're headed to Harvard in the fall, right? That's where Harry went." This got his attention. He was absolutely dying for some more detailed information on school.

"Really? Well why didn't you lead with that, Jack? Harry, I don't mean to put you on the spot, but I'd like you to tell me absolutely everything."

Harry, it turned out, was very much up to the task. He captivated the two younger boys with about an hour's worth of tales. He had studied literature, in particular the collecting of old books, and now worked directly with libraries and helped them collect old books. In fact, he was just returning home from a book-buying trip in Europe.

Dick was fascinated by Harry's stories of clubs and classes, literature and history. When he talked about books, he beamed with excitement. His passion was enough to make anyone hang on the edge of their seat. It was a sensation that Dick had only felt before when he had heard his father talk about great old tennis matches.

"Do you have your books with you?" he asked, almost surprising himself with his curiosity.

"Of course, but I don't show them to anyone," Harry said seriously.

"I can't believe you keep them in a safe," Jack teased, looking to Dick to follow along – the two boys were used to taunting people together, ever since they were kids.

But Dick was in no mood for teasing. There was something intriguing about the glimmer in Harry's eye when he spoke. He was determined to find out exactly what it was.

This was by far the worst dinner Karl had ever had.

While most would have considered the food a delicacy, Karl was having a hard time not getting sick at the table. An appetizer course of oysters, followed by salmon with cucumber and mousseline sauce as an entrée was a bit more than his meat-and-potatoes stomach had bargained for. That's probably why Sallie Beckwith insisted he order it. "It takes a *fine man* to appreciate perfect seafood, Mr. Behr, and what better place to get seafood than on the sea?"

The challenges she could come up with were downright ridiculous, but Karl wasn't about to back down now. He would do practically anything at this point to win her over. He had learned from his travels with her not to avoid her games, but rather to take her on as though he were playing the great Maurice McLoughlin himself. Of course, playing Mac had never made him actually vomit. He wasn't sure how well that would go over.

It was far from just the copious amounts of seafood, though, that were making the current meal unpleasant. Sallie was putting him on the spot every chance she got and he was not handling it very well. His bow tie felt like it was about to choke him. The lights from the overpriced chandelier felt like spotlights trained right on him. His suit felt tight, no doubt from overindulging while in his melancholic state in Vienna. And he was seated as far away from Helen at the table as was physically possible. Sallie was admirably meticulous. Joining them at the table was Helen's stepfather, Richard Beckwith, Edwin and Gertrude Kimball, Frank and Anna Warren, and two other couples whom Karl was certain had been recruited for the sole purpose of putting more distance between himself and Helen.

He had met up with Helen earlier in the day while Sallie was getting a beauty treatment at the parlor, another luxury afforded to those in first class. She had told him that Karl's surprise appearance on board the *Titanic* had gone over just about as they should have expected. Sallie was absolutely livid and insisted that Helen would be too busy with social engagements and other activities on board the ship to have any time at all to spend with him. It wasn't true of course, and there was no way for her to keep her nineteen-year-old daughter in sight at all times, but the pronouncement didn't bode well.

Helen had somehow managed to insist that Karl be allowed to eat dinner with them, but now it had become obvious that the only reason Sallie had agreed to such a notion was so that she would have the opportunity to humiliate him in a public setting.

"Mr. Behr, I'm surprised you made the ship at all. I know that timeliness is not your best trait." That had been her greeting to Karl, a blatant reference to a couple of months earlier when he and Helen had been half an hour late for departure from Algiers, delaying the entire ship. It had been an honest mistake on Karl's part – he was simply so elated to have Helen to himself that he forgot to keep an eye on the clock – but it had just added to Sallie's list of strikes against him.

Karl had of course come to dinner with grand plans to present his gifts to Sallie and Richard and win them over with his charm and charisma, but he found himself in a situation he was not able to control. He wasn't used to dealing with people not liking him. His entire life he'd been the handsome, popular and talented one, able to win over any room he was in with quiet confidence and a smile. Sure, his older brothers gave him a hard time often and his father wasn't particularly gushing with praise, but other than old-fashioned teasing he had never had anyone outright dislike him. Sallie could be so forward with her antagonism at times that it completely knocked him off balance.

It was an atrocious feeling, this insecurity and lack of confidence. He had heard Gertie talk about it from time to time in her teen years, when she was going through a particularly awkward phase and was feeling like she would never fit in with any friends. He would listen to her, as a good brother did, glad that she felt comfortable opening up to him in such a way, but he never really understood what it felt like to not fit in. Whether it had been because of his natural ability with tennis, his looks, or just something about his personality, he had never had a problem in social situations.

He had studiously practiced his introductions in the vanity mirror in his stateroom earlier that evening, going through his approach to the table, where he would smoothly take Mrs. Beckwith's hand and kiss her glove with a friendly "pleased to see you again," followed by a simple "You look exquisite tonight." Before she could even get in a snide remark he would have her eating out of the palm of his hands. The presents would be the icing on the cake. By the dessert course they would be practically begging him to marry Helen.

Of course the moment he entered the dining room, already uncomfortable thanks to the snugness of his suit, and saw Mrs. Beckwith glaring at him, he froze. Instead, he spent dinner brushing passive (and not-so-passive) aggressive remarks off his shoulder and staring at his silverware.

The dinner became more and more uncomfortable as time went on. Everyone at the table was made uncomfortable by Mrs. Beckwith's snide remarks. The tension was as thick as the mousseline. Occasionally, Karl would be able to look down to the end of the table and catch a glimpse of Helen, who as usual looked stunning. Her dress was red, the color of love and desire, a perfect reminder for him why he was here. She was wearing matching red lipstick, something he had never seen on her, and at times it took all of his control not to just run around the table and kiss her right there, both to satisfy his urges and to enrage her mother.

Instead, he listened to the small talk that the rest of the table engaged in and observed the company around him. The

Kimballs were a particularly intriguing pair. From what he could gather from the enthralling conversation going on at the table Mr. Kimball owned a piano shop, and it made perfect sense seeing as he and his wife were dressed head to toe in black and white. Something told Karl that this wasn't merely a coincidence, but that this was something they did on a regular basis. They even had voices that sounded like opposing ends of the piano keyboard. Gertrude Kimball had a voice like a mouse squeaking, whereas Edwin Kimball spoke in a deep baritone, a tone so low that it sounded like it must be a strain on the voice to even attempt to reach it.

Gertrude and Sallie were the same age, but you would never know it by looking at them. Gertrude looked old enough to be Sallie's mother. Not that she was looking rundown, but rather, as much as Karl hated to admit it, Sallie cut a marvelous figure. She was slightly taller and wider than Helen, but other than that they could have been mistaken for twins. She was radiant enough, when she wasn't plotting against her daughter's suitor, to win the heart of a man ten years her junior, which in fact she had done with the quiet but charming Richard Beckwith. Richard was a kind man who, although he refused to meddle in his wife's dealings with Karl, had always been as friendly as could be himself, to the extent that Karl had even imagined Richard a potential ally in his cause.

On this particular evening, however, there was nothing even Richard could have done. There was nothing anyone could do. Sallie snuck insults into the small talk over and over again. It took every ounce of self control for Karl to keep down the fish and keep his temper intact and just make it through dinner. His family's adhesive business was belittled, his tennis failures enumerated, and by the end of the meal he was feeling like he was back in Vienna. All he wanted to do was grab a whiskey and retreat to his cabin.

"Mr. Behr, do you care to join us in the smoking room?" Mr. Kimball asked after the meal with a pang of sympathy in his eye.

"Thank you sir, but I'm quite exhausted. I think I'm just going to head back to my room. Thank you for having me to dinner." He knew he should seek out Mrs. Beckwith personally for a thank you, knew he should bring out the presents, knew that he should do absolutely anything to try and salvage the evening but he was completely disheartened and disappointed with himself.

Helen came to him, putting her hand on his shoulder and looking him in the eye, a look of great concern. "Do you want to go for a walk?" she offered. He did, but he felt as if she would want to rehash the evening, and he didn't have it in him.

"You should spend some time with your mother. I'm just going to get some rest, I'll see you tomorrow." He kissed her on the cheek quickly, nodded to the rest of the table and walked away.

This was going to be harder than he thought.

It was a fun, uneventful day for Dick. He went to the gym, did some reading and survived another dinner and smoking room session without getting into much trouble. He fell asleep quickly and didn't stir until dawn when the first hint of sunshine shot through their porthole. He looked over to his father's bed but didn't see him there. He sat up in bed, startled for a moment that something was wrong. Almost immediately, though, he saw his father standing by the porthole, staring out at the water, just smiling.

It was a smile he had never seen come over his father. This wasn't how he smiled in public. This was a peaceful, quiet smile. One of those grins that you could actually see coming from inside a person. But even more notable than that was the fact that he was perfectly, completely still.

"Pop? You okay"

"Shhhhh. Just come look."

Dick stumbled out of bed and joined his father. He was taken aback by the view from the porthole. The sun was rising over the ocean, its oblique rays reflected in the crystal clear waters. The ship was gliding through the water seamlessly, securely, sensationally.

The two men stood there in complete silence, neither one of them seeming to have any desire to let the moment pass.

"We made it son," said Charles. "We made it."

Dick didn't know what to say. His eyes kept glancing back and forth between the porthole and his father's unfamiliar, serene face. Those were not words he ever expected to hear from his father. Maybe if Dick ever won the U.S. Nationals or reached the top of the national rankings. Maybe then he would say those words. But here they were, just beginning their journey. Dick had yet to even win a tennis match on American soil.

He looked closely at his father for what felt like the first time. Dick spent the better part of his days observing others, watching their every move, but he realized at that moment that he never stopped to study his father. He heard his father, he felt his love, his perfectionism, his expectations, but did he ever really see him?

Charles was a man who had gone far beyond what the world had expected of him. He was a painfully short man who had been battling illnesses since the day he was born, though Dick was never very clear on what exactly those illnesses were. He had lines all over his face, far more than a fifty-one-year-old should have, but since he typically had a smile on his face they were rarely noticed. Sometimes Dick wondered if his father's outgoing personality was some sort of overcompensation for his health and physical stature. There was so much Dick had yet to understand. There were so many mysteries left to be solved. He was disappointed at how little he really knew his father despite their apparent closeness. He suddenly realized that he was reaching out to his father – literally, instinctively, putting his arm around him.

He had not planned this. In fact, he wasn't sure he had ever done this in private before. It was an instinct, like a shot you didn't know you could hit until you did it. Dick realized that touching of any kind usually made him either cringe or giggle, but this was somehow different. This felt necessary, overdue, comforting.

The butterflies in his stomach settled and as his father reached his arm around Dick too. He couldn't help feel that this was something they both needed. In a sea of change and uncertainty, they each needed something familiar to hold onto.

6

Karl enjoyed a leisurely morning, sleeping in a bit and ordering breakfast to his room so that he would avoid any more run-ins with Sallie Beckwith. But when he heard a knock on his door and saw Helen's smiling face staring back at him through the peephole. He was elated. "I know you're in there, Mr. Behr!" she called through the door. "Stop primping and open up!"

Karl opened up the door and Helen barreled into his arms, nearly knocking him over.

"Well good morning to you!" he exclaimed, attempting to match her enthusiasm though it was difficult for him at this hour.

"Good morning sleepyhead, I missed you at breakfast this morning," she said, gazing into his eyes in a way that made him forget his own name.

"I missed you too." He leaned in to kiss her and immediately forgot about the events from the previous evening.

"So why didn't you come to breakfast?"

"I figured after last night I was better off dining alone. I don't know if I'm able to handle any more of those onslaughts." Just thinking about it made him shudder.

"Oh Karl, don't be so dramatic. It wasn't *that* bad."

Karl glared at her in disbelief, wondering if they were even talking about the same dinner.

"Okay, my mother was not on her best behavior, but I really don't think it was a total disaster."

She moved away from him, prancing around his room examining all the details. Since the whirlwind of the first day Karl had started to love his room. It had every amenity he could ever ask for: a wash station, a dresser and a lovely closet, even a plush chair to sit in and read. He was sure that there were far more extravagant staterooms in first class, but this was well and above the standards of all other rooms he'd ever had aboard a ship. The walls were white and everything had a gold trim that made him feel a bit like royalty. It made him proud to be able to afford such accommodations on his own. He wished his father were there to see it.

Of course, the stewardess had not yet been in, so it was a bit of a mess, which was the first thing Helen teased him about. She picked up his night clothes, which were lying in a pile on the floor and threw them at him.

"Why Mr. Behr, you are on board the finest ship there ever was and you still can't pick up after yourself?"

"Why should I? I have you to do that," he said, grinning wide and knowing that even though he was obviously teasing he had an earful of a reply coming to him. Helen was not the type of woman who would ever accept that her purpose in life was simply to take care of a man and Karl was well aware of that.

"I don't even have the time to dignify that with a response. Hurry up, I have someone I want you to meet!"

"But I was hoping you would just want to stay here with me all day long."

"Where did I ever find you?" Helen teased. "But really, hurry up. I met the most fascinating two women this morning at breakfast, a mother and daughter. My mom is in the spa all morning and I told them that we would meet them for tea."

Leave it to Helen to make new friends before ten in the morning. Though sharing her with anyone didn't sound appealing to Karl at all, the news that her mother would not be joining them was enough to put a pep in his step. He threw on his vest, Helen straightened his hair a bit and she grabbed his hand and led him out to meet the mystery guests.

"So who are these people?" Karl asked as they ascended the Grand Staircase to the B Deck where the Café Parisian was located, where he assumed they were going.

"You'll never believe it Karl. You know how I've been telling you about the suffragist movement in England that has been so active? Well, I met two women at breakfast this morning who have been a big part of it: Edith and Elise Chibnall, or Bowerman, I'm not sure what they're going by now because of marriages. But anyway, I've read about them in the papers. I just couldn't believe it when I ran into Edith this morning. Elise is just a few years older than me. Oh, and get this, they practically fainted when I told them you were on the ship with me. They're huge tennis fans and were at Wimbledon in 1907 and saw you play in the doubles final!"

Karl liked the sound of this. He loved hearing Helen talk politics. He was thrilled that she had something she was so passionate about. It was part of what made her such a strong woman. And he could use some fan adulation right about now, especially after the previous night.

Edith and Elise reminded him a lot of Helen. They were both full of life, humble and passionate about their pursuits. Though they didn't look as similar as most mother and daughter pairings – they had identical mannerisms, moving their hands and inflecting their voices in identical patterns.

They were charming and engaging and looked directly in Karl's eyes when they talked to him – but with warmth, not with daggers like Mrs. Beckwith did.

"Mr. Behr! What an honor it is to meet you," Edith said when they were introduced. It was a while since he was greeted in such a manner. He was fairly well known for his tennis prowess in the United States but was far from a celebrity. It took a select group of people to recognize him or be honored by his presence, even among tennis followers he was overshadowed by more prominent players in America such as William Larned and recently Maurice McLoughlin.

"Mr. Behr, we have such fond memories of you playing doubles with Mr. Wright in 1907. We were so pleased when you were able to follow your Wimbledon success with a victory over the Australasian team in Davis Cup."

"Well, a doubles victory, you mean. I'm afraid we couldn't quite handle Brookes and Wilding that year in the singles and make it to the Challenge Round against your own British team."

"Yes, of course, and I can't promise you that we could have cheered for you against our Arthur Gore. But against the Australasians you had our fondest hopes."

"That is mighty nice of you Mrs. Chibnall. And please call me Karl."

"Then we insist you call us Edith and Elise. How is your tennis progressing these days? Will you be coming back to Wimbledon this summer?"

"Well, I've been a little distracted lately..." Karl said with a laugh, nodding towards Helen who was looking at him lovingly. "But I believe I still have a few good runs left in me. I am excited for the summer."

"He's been practicing so much, I wouldn't be surprised if he won Newport this year," Helen said, clearly relishing the chance to brag about her beau.

"Well, Karl, you certainly do have a special lady here. Helen, you mentioned this morning that you had been quite involved with the movement in New York. Would you mind telling us more?" For someone who looked just about Helen's age Elise had the confidence and vocabulary of someone a generation older. Karl hadn't often seen Helen uncomfortable, but he could tell that she was a bit intimidated by the situation. He had to say she was adorable when flustered.

"Oh, I'm sure I have led you to believe I'm more involved than I actually am. I certainly am a big believer in the suffragist movement and have become involved at my school in New York, but I've done nothing like what you two have done in England."

"Well, Helen, you are young and passionate and the movement could certainly use more people like you. If you'd like I could introduce you to some people. I can see the two of you are going to be quite the influential couple."

Helen glowed with enthusiasm. They sat for the rest of the morning listening to the Chibnalls talk about the petitions, rallies and protests they had been a part of over the past four years, telling stories of arrests and injury, defeat and victory. Karl kept thinking about the words "influential couple." In the Chibnalls' presence, he could actually believe it.

Though there were many luxuries that made the *Titanic* stand out from other ships, Dick's favorite was the gym. He enjoyed being active and getting in a good sweat. He also loved how all of the machines worked and was fascinated by the intricacies of the bike and the way different weights worked. He felt there was a science behind working out that nobody else fully understood.

The gym was also another place where he and his father could bond. His father was always in there with him. It was a part of exercise they both took very seriously, but it was intimate because it was just the two of them.

He and Charles entered the gym at 2:00 p.m., right when it opened for the men – it was reserved for women in the morning — and were greeted by the enthusiastic gym attendant, Thomas McCawley. Dick had made good friends with him the previous day when he stopped by with Harry and Jack. Thomas was Scottish, in his mid thirties, and knew everything there was to know about the equipment. He also kept it all in tip-top shape, making sure the exercise bikes were running smoothly and the weights were in perfect order. Of course most of the people on the *Titanic* who used the gymnasium did so mainly for show, or to have another place to socialize and gossip — as if there weren't enough places to do that — so he was thrilled when Dick came in wanting to talk in depth about all of the equipment. He even took great humor out of Charles when he barreled in and took the place over, asking Thomas a thousand questions and second-guessing the placement of equipment.

He called Dick and Charles his "favorite passengers" and although Dick suspected he said that to everyone, it still somehow meant something coming from Thomas. He took pride in the gym, which was like another home to him. He always had a smile on his face. He had two children, whose photographs he displayed proudly.

He had seen some tennis matches at Wimbledon and he and Charles could spend hours discussing the merits of the various players they had seen – from the brothers Reggie and Laurie Doherty from Britain to the Australasians Wilding and Brookes. His tennis knowledge rivaled Charles's and it was actually fun for Dick to listen to them talk.

Dick and Charles were dressed in their white flannels and cardigans and sat next to each other on the exercise bikes. They frequently used their time in the gym as time to prepare for tennis matches. While Dick was riding the bike, his father would take out his moleskin and discuss the myriad of subjects and players documented on the pages. There was a give and take to their relationship in the gym, a rhythm, a purpose. They were a team. Today, though, they exercised side-by-side in a relaxed silence, looking through the windows in the gym that faced the deck of the ship. It was an enjoyable respite for Dick, and allowed him to momentarily forget about the questions and doubts that were plaguing him. Of course, the silence didn't last for very long.

"Charles Duane Williams! I don't believe it, is that really you?"

A man in a colorful pinstripe suit and cane burst into the gymnasium, interrupting the quiet. Dick could tell that his father recognized the loud and eccentric man instantly, as Charles leapt up off of his exercise bike and greeted the man with a bear hug. The two instantly began enthusiastically chatting and within minutes Dick knew seemingly everything there was to know about this man. His name was William Dulles, a prominent lawyer and horse breeder from Philadelphia. He was a bachelor travelling alone with only his beloved French bulldog, who he was excitedly entering in the *Titanic* dog show on Monday.

Charles, of course, easily matched Mr. Dulles's enthusiasm.

"William, you have to meet my son Richard Norris. My boy is an excellent tennis player. I think that one day he could win the U.S. Nationals!"

"Is that right? Well, I feel honored to be in the presence of greatness then. It is a pleasure to meet you son."

Dick got up off the bike and endured a crushing handshake from Mr. Dulles, though he longed for the quiet of moments before. He disliked when his father said such things and placed expectations on him, although he knew it was coming from a good place. Charles put in his best effort in everything he did. He worked hard and enjoyed life more than anyone else Dick had ever met. He expected the same from his son and he truly believed that Dick was championship material. These weren't empty promises he was throwing around to impress his friends.

"Good for you boys for getting a workout! I was just getting caught up on my reading."

Mr. Dulles had in his hands a copy of the *Atlantic Daily Bulletin*, a daily newspaper the *Titanic* printed for its passengers.

"So, boys, what do you think about the upcoming election? Do you think Roosevelt will really create a new party?" Mr. Dulles asked them.

It was a presidential election year in the United States and the Republican Party was divided. Incumbent President William Taft was trying to secure the nomination from his party, but former President Teddy Roosevelt was running against him in the primary elections. At the end of March in Chicago, Roosevelt stated that he would run for office whether he got the nomination from the Republican Party or not. This threatened to divide the Republican Party between conservatives and progressives and was a frequent political topic of conversation on board the *Titanic*.

"I don't know. It seems like the Republican Party is in a quagmire. Roosevelt's speech in Illinois surely was foreboding," Charles said. "I must say that I do like Roosevelt as he shares our passion for tennis and is a big supporter of the sport."

"I imagine if Roosevelt does run separate from the Republican Party, it could create an opportunity for the Democrats and we might be looking at President Woodrow Wilson or President Champ Clark. What about you Richard, what does our future champion think of the current Presidential landscape?" Mr. Dulles asked.

Dick disliked political talk almost as much as he hated being put on the spot. The truth is, he wasn't as well-versed on the current political climate as he would like to be and was still forming his opinion. Times were uncertain in the United States. He could sympathize.

"The truth is Mr. Dulles, I am uncertain at this time and I would like to gather as much information as I can before making an educated decision or opinion. It will be quite interesting to see how it all sorts out," Dick said, choosing to be honest rather than blindly carry on a conversation.

"Well, Richard Norris! What a refreshing answer. You know, I think it's just fine for a man your age to be unsure of a few things. You have plenty of time to figure it out." Mr. Dulles said enthusiastically.

Dick was unsure about so many things these days. He sincerely hoped that Mr. Dulles was right.

—◦/◦/◦—

Mrs. Beckwith had arranged a private dinner for her and Helen, so Karl planned on dining alone in his room and then heading to the smoking room to try and make some headway with Mr. Beckwith. After all, despite the fact that Karl had traveled with him for ten full days in Europe it seemed as if he had not spent any time alone with him. He hoped that he could somehow reach Mrs. Beckwith through her husband. It certainly couldn't hurt.

He headed into the smoking room around nine in the evening and had the familiar feeling upon entering that he was in foreign territory without a plan. He hadn't been invited to join anyone there, and considering he had turned down their invitation the previous night, it was completely possible that he was persona non grata.

He didn't recognize anyone when he came in and took a seat at the bar. It was not long before his peace was broken.

"Hey, hey, hey. Don't I know you? Aren't you that tennis player?" asked a man at the bar.

Karl absolutely couldn't believe it. Mr. Beckwith and Mr. Kimball were nowhere in sight. All he wanted to do was have a quiet drink at the bar and here he was getting recognized for the second time in the day. He was practically *never* recognized. Things just would not go his way.

Karl sat at the bar, trying to ignore this man, wondering the best way to handle the situation. He could walk out completely, but then he might miss Mr. Beckwith and Mr. Kimball if they came in.

"I was there last year in Newport when Little beat you. My God, you were so close to winning that match you must have thought it was yours, and then you really just gave out. I mean, you just couldn't manage to win another point, it seemed."

"Thank you so much."

Of course he remembered the match. It had been soon after he'd started seeing Helen and everything he did was in the hope of impressing her. He'd had a good summer of tennis and was back in the top ten of the rankings for the first time in over a year, a status he was very proud of. Though he had not won a title in Newport or as a member of the U.S. Davis Cup team, he had been ranked as high as third in the United States back in 1907 and still felt that he would be able to win the big title some day. Because of his work at school and then with his father, he didn't have as much time to devote to the sport as some of the other top players of the day did. But he took a lot of pride in his fitness and his fight – they made up for his lack of perfect shot selection and ability.

The match that the bar patron was talking about had been a particularly gut-wrenching defeat for him. It was the first time that Helen had seen him play a match. She and Gertie made the journey from Briarcliff to Newport, six hours by train, and they were seated in the front row of the packed grandstand. Karl was playing against Raymond Little, a good friend and one of his toughest competitors. One of Karl's best memories in tennis had come against Little in the semifinals at Newport in 1906, one of Karl's best years ever in tennis. He had just burst onto the scene the year before, whereas Little was considered one of the contenders to win the tournament.

Karl stunned the Newport crowds with the best tennis of his life, upsetting the future champion William Larned in the second round and storming all the way to the semifinals. There he found himself down two sets to one, but that's where the fitness and fight kicked in. Seven times in the fourth set Little had match point and seven times Karl refused to lose the point. Each time the crowd roared, though still certain that Little would soon finish it off. But that fourth-set finish never happened. Karl stuck it out 11-9 and went on to win a tight fifth set 6-4. There was no telling what could happen if you never gave up. That great comeback victory had come to mind more than once as Karl had pondered his seemingly impossible task of winning over Sally Beckwith.

Of course, this past year the tables had turned. Karl was now the favorite in the match against Little, whom the experts had labeled over the hill, his best tennis far behind him. Helen was there, in the front row, and Karl had no doubt he was going to beat Little again and ride far into the tournament. It was the fourth round and he was one of the contenders for the title. What greater way to woo the love of one's life than to hold the National Championship trophy high as she watched from the front row?

But Raymond Little had other plans. Before Karl knew it, he lost the first set 6-0. For all he knew Helen was wondering why she had traveled six hours to watch Karl lose such a one-sided affair. Little was playing the most inspired tennis he had in years and fought off his resurgent opponent in the second set 10-8 to take a two–sets-to-love lead. Karl set his jaw and began one of his signature comebacks, taking the next two sets 8-6 and then 6-1. It finally seemed clear – with full control of momentum – he was on his way to the next round. But the thirty-one-year-old Little showed some fight of his own and held off Behr 6-4 in the final set. It had been crushing for many reasons, mainly because Karl was the one who ran out of gas and he had to wonder if he could ever again compete for a championship or if he was going to have to resign himself to the fact that his best days were far behind him. He also felt that he had let down Helen. Though she was nothing but supportive, he couldn't help but feel that he disappointed her.

So it was wrenching that here in the middle of the sea, as he fiddled with the engagement ring he feared would become a long-term resident in his pocket, he was forced to endure a rehashing of every point of that devastating loss.

"After you took the fourth set, everyone thought the match was yours. But I could see you'd just burned your last quart of fuel. I turned to my wife and I said, 'I don't think he can do it. His legs are gone.' And I was right! Your legs had left you. You made it to four-all in the fifth, but I don't think you won a point after that!"

Karl glared at him and nodded, clutching his whiskey tight and wondering how he could extricate himself from this conversation without being too rude. He hadn't said a word but it hardly mattered to this pest. How long would he persist in having a conversation with himself?

A tap on his shoulder brought Karl back to reality. He was as elated as he was flustered when he turned around to see Richard Beckwith standing there, a whimsical grin on his face as always, his tall top hat a bit crooked and his bow tie loosened.

"Fine sir," he said to Karl's unwanted companion. "Do you mind if we steal Mr. Behr for a bit?"

Without waiting for an answer the two men were off, walking over to join Mr. Kimball in a reserved group of plush chairs in the corner.

"Thank you Mr. Beckwith. You really got me out of a bind there."

"Call me Richard, son. And don't mention it. I figured you had dealt with enough hassling on this trip to last a lifetime."

Karl wasn't quite sure how to react to this, wanting to express his gratitude but at the same time unwilling to admit any annoyance with Mrs. Beckwith. Instead, he decided it would be the perfect time to finally unveil his gift.

"Oh Mr. Beckwith, err, I mean, Richard. I picked you up some cigars in Paris. I remember you saying in Algiers that you had a difficult time finding these."

Karl handed over the cigars. Richard laughed.

"I can't believe you remembered these. You are a fine young man, Mr. Behr. Just hang in there, do you hear me? Your time will come."

Karl collapsed in a leather chair across from Richard, smiling as the words soaked in. He was a fine man. And he could do more than hang in there.

After dinner, Dick and Jack managed to escape the smoking room and they were hanging out with the rest of the younger crowd in the Café Parisian. Harry decided he wanted to stay behind – Jack teased that he just wanted to head back to his room and check on his precious books in his safe. There were some drinks flowing, bridge games going and the orchestra could be heard playing from the deck. Occasionally, a particular lively couple would get up and dance, but mainly everyone was just mingling. Young girls and boys were flirting all around. Dick and Jack watched and enjoyed.

The Cafe Parisian was a lot of fun in the evenings. True to its name, it felt just like you were dining on a sidewalk café on the streets of Paris. There was pine flooring, white walls with ivy extending to the ceiling, comfortable wicker furniture. Most importantly, there were huge windows so you could look right out onto the deck, see the water and be reminded that you were out at sea. For better or worse, in the confines of the dining room and smoking room this was an easy thing to forget.

Dick and Jack managed to secure a table to themselves and were just sitting back and taking in the scenes. They could have asked to join in on a game of bridge or tried to engage one of many of the eligible ladies in conversation, but they were both happier just sitting back and observing. This was one reason Dick enjoyed Jack's company so much.

Bored after a while, though, Jack began flicking some rolled-up pieces of paper from his pocket, trying to get them stuck in the ivy.

"Your father would be mighty proud if he could see you now," Dick laughed, but eventually joined in too. Occasionally they would miss their mark and a piece of paper would land on the brim of one of the enormous hats the girls were wearing, an occurrence which left the two boys in stitches, particularly since nobody seemed to notice. They were carrying on like thirteen-year-olds and not caring one whit.

"What sort of trouble are you boys getting into here?"

A familiar voice startled them: Major Archibald Butt, chief

military aide to the president, and Francis Millet, one of the world's eminent painters, were watching them and asking to sit down at their table.

The boys tried haplessly to hide evidence of their game. Dick scrambled, stood up and pulled out a chair for the major, a rather awkward and unnecessary move.

"Why thank you Mr. Williams, we just needed to get out of the smoking room. It's good for old fellows like us to be around the youngsters from time to time."

"And despite what the doctors say, the smoke really isn't good for one's health," Millet added.

"Well, that too," Major Butt said with a chuckle.

"We're pleased to have you both join us," Jack said, looking at Dick with eyes that screamed *How do we handle this situation?* The two boys had hoped to escape adult society for an evening, not be caught in the middle of it.

Mr. Millett pulled a little piece of paper out of his pocket and crumpled it up.

"What are the rules, boys?" he said with a grin. "Is the aim the ivy or the hats? It was difficult to tell by watching you two in action."

Dick and Jack both blushed but burst out in laughter when, in unison, Mr. Millett and Major Butt flicked pieces of paper into the same brim of a particularly large hat.

How old are you, Mr. Williams, if you don't mind me asking?"

"I'm twenty-one."

"Aaah, that is a fine age, isn't it, Francis? You have your whole life in front of you, boy. When I was your age I was on my way to being a journalist, can you believe that? I worked for the *Louisville Courier-Journal.*"

"Really? I always wanted to become a journalist!" Jack spoke up with such excitement that it completely took Dick by surprise. All Jack had been doing since the men had arrived, as far as Dick could tell, was visibly attempting to squelch his own imminent fits of laughter. With this outburst, however, Dick realized he didn't have the slightest idea what Jack's ambitions were. Such conversations about life ambitions were exactly what he and Jack were always trying to avoid.

"For God's sake, don't encourage him, Archie," said Mr. Millet, rolling his eyes and laughing.

"Well Mr. Thayer, I'm afraid I do not recommend journalism as a profession to any young man. It is comprised of windbags who haven't the slightest idea what they are talking about and I was about the worst offender. Thank goodness I finally realized my folly and took a commission in the army at the ripe old age of thirty-five. Have either of you boys thought about joining the army? We could use a couple of fine young men such as yourselves."

Dick and Jack looked at each other, trying to stay calm. They were both very well aware of Major Archibald Butt's achievements – he was not only *involved* in the army, he'd been the chief military aide to both President Roosevelt and President Taft and was surely one of the best military minds on the planet. Dick had always had a fascination with the military and politics. He had always thought that serving one's country would be the highest honor. It was difficult to discuss such things with his father, since Charles's health had prevented him from serving, so Dick had always kept such thoughts to himself. Besides, who had time for the army when there was so much tennis to be played? But hearing the

Major discuss it reignited his interest.

"It would be an honor to join the army, sir," Dick responded, deepening his voice a bit. Jack just nodded along, trying to recover from his humiliating confession.

"Well boys, I do hope if you ever get the chance to do so that you will serve your country. Now, what would you say the odds are I could get this piece of paper into that fine gentlemen's top hat over in the corner?"

Major Butt pointed to the corner where a particularly boisterous young man was loudly flirting with a girl who didn't seem to be interested in the least.

"I think you can do it sir," Jack said eagerly, but the Major didn't need the encouragement. He lined up, flicked the paper and landed it directly in the center of the hat, nodding confidently.

7

It was two days before the big squash match. Charles had reserved some practice time early in the morning, at a very unfavorable hour for Dick to be up and moving, let alone practicing.

Dick was still not that enthusiastic about this squash game against Mr. Thayer, but his father never engaged in anything half-heartedly and continued to try to instill this trait to his son. Charles was almost silly with his eagerness for this match, fully embracing the sporting challenge and fun that would be had between his son and his good friend. Dick soaked in his father's zealous morning fervor, but it was still hard to drown out other thoughts in his head. Dick felt that the events of the last few days, from running into Karl Behr on the train, to meeting Harry Widener, to Major Archibald Butt himself encouraging him to join the army, were trying to tell him something, but he just wasn't sure what. These thoughts were far too heavy for so early in the morning. Dick knew that if he didn't fix his attention to the task at hand, he was going to have his head knocked all over the squash court. Though squash shared a lot of the same shots and terminology as tennis, it was a completely different sport. He had played some, and certainly his racket skills from tennis came in handy, but what if Mr. Thayer were more of a squash expert than he let on? Of course, he'd never let anyone know that he was worried.

"Bend your knees, son. You have to anticipate the ball, get

back to the T in the center as soon as you can after every shot. There you go!"

"Son, when the ball comes at you that hard you have to mix it up, change up the pace a little, just like you would if you were playing McLoughlin and his cannon serve. Absorb the pace on the return."

Naturally his father had found a way to bring McLoughlin into the conversation. The man was relentless. Maurice McLoughlin had recently become some sort of obsession for Charles, despite the fact that neither of them had ever met him or seen him play tennis. But apparently "the California Comet," as the press was calling him, was the new face of tennis, and from what he had read and heard from Charles's many sources, he had pretty much revolutionized the game with his strategy of hitting tremendously hard serves (hence his nickname) and running right up to the net behind them. "Serve and volley," they called it. Charles had spent the past few months working with Dick to perfect a return of serve that he thought would minimize the effectiveness of such a strategy. McLoughlin was ranked second behind Bill Larned in the U.S. rankings for 1911 and won the all-comers' draw that year at Newport, losing in the Challenge Round to Larned, the holder. Charles was sure that the road to the national title in 1912 – and for years to come – led right through "the California Comet."

Thud. Whack.

"Not like that Richard Norris. Aim higher!"

Dick really should have been out on the court practicing sooner than two days before the match. He found it funny that his father had suddenly become a squash expert.

Thud. Whack.

"Get back to the T!"

Thud. Whack.

"Come on! Move your feet Richard Norris!"

Thud. WHACK.

On the last shot Dick hit the squash ball with all of his might. Had he been on a tennis court, the ball would have hit the back barrier on the fly like a cannonball. The ball ricocheted around the court and he burst out into laughter. Charles was not amused.

"Pops, don't worry. I'll be able to handle Mr. Thayer."

You are a fine young man. Hang in there.

The words from Mr. Beckwith the previous night gave Karl such a spring in his step on this beautiful day that he felt like a completely different man. After getting some time to canoodle with Helen on the deck of the ship, visiting the barber shop and joining Helen and the Chibnalls for tea again, Karl was ready to face Mrs. Beckwith. He would be joining them all for dinner again, two nights after the seafood debacle. This time, although one could say he was down a set or two, he was certain that he was going to make a spirited comeback.

In his cabin, he fixed his bow tie and put on the finest suit he had. He even slicked back his hair a little bit, a look that he knew Helen loathed but that was sure to make him look more presentable to her mother. After all, that was how his late mother had liked his hair.

Karl thought back to that first day he met Helen, when he invited her for a walk in the cold winter air. He never knew that conversation with anyone, let alone a beautiful woman, could be that effortless. He didn't know that it was possible to connect with anyone so intimately in such a short amount of time. There was no such thing as small talk between them. They teased each other mercilessly, joyfully, but mainly they shared the deepest and darkest parts of their pasts with each other without a single hint of judgment.

One of the common experiences that bonded them so tightly was the loss of a parent. Helen's father died when she was a young girl and Karl's mother passed away from pneumonia in December of 1907. Somehow with Helen, a girl he had just met, he was able to open up about his grief and confusion and his worry for his father. And in turn, he listened to her talk about the months after her father died so unexpectedly, when she and her mother and brother were awash in sorrow. Even now he found it hard to believe anyone as strong as Helen or, in her own way, Mrs. Beckwith needing to cling to anyone out of grief, but perhaps that was part of why he loved Helen so much. He knew that vulnerability was there. He knew that despite her politics and her fierce independence that she did need others, just like everyone else. He wanted to make sure that he would be there for her when she needed him.

He felt for the ring once more. In his head he went over the speech he had prepared again, assured that he had found the perfect mix of confidence, gratitude and humility. Surely once Mrs. Beckwith listened to him and heard what a perfect combination of athletic accomplishment and business ambition he presented and how perfect he was for Helen, she would find that all of her objections to him would fade away like sea mist. Then, later that night, he was going to take Helen out on the promenade, underneath the stars and propose. This was it.

Karl strutted into the dining room right on time, three minutes after the bell had rung just as he had planned. He most certainly did not want to be late. Sure enough as he entered the room, the Beckwiths and Kimballs were just arriving at their table.

Helen saw Karl first, and while he had hoped she would run over to him and leap into his arms the way she had the first night on the ship, he accepted her beaming smile as a seal of approval for his slick hairdo and purposeful stride. He was doing this for them, finally stepping out on the limb he should have trod back in Algiers.

"Mrs. Beckwith. Thank you so much for having me to dinner tonight. I have brought you a token of my affection."

He started his greeting a few feet too soon before everyone had even noticed he was present and stuck his gift out with a bit too much gusto. But he accomplished his first goal, which was to have the first word. He looked over at Helen who seemed pleased. At least, that was how he interpreted her expression.

"Well, Mr. Behr, thank you. But you certainly shouldn't have, especially since you don't have anything for our other guests. I shall open it in private later so as not to be rude."

He hadn't seen that answer coming. She was always full of surprises. Still, he would be able to recover from this. Merely an unexpected break of serve early in the first set. She hadn't heard his prepared speech yet, so he knew he could recover. He looked over at Mr. Beckwith, who was still smiling and wearing his crooked top hat, and took his seat, which was once again located as far away from Helen as possible. He couldn't help but wish that his sister Gertie was there. She would know exactly how to calm him down and encourage him to begin his speech. They had often concocted similar plans as children when they wanted to get something from their parents.

The dinner seemed to go on forever. Mr. Kimball rambled on about the piano business. Mrs. Beckwith told them all about her conversation earlier in the day with the managing director of White Star Line, Bruce Ismay. Helen spoke enthusiastically about her lunch with the Chibnalls. Karl listened intently, waiting for the perfect opportunity to speak up. He snuck smiles at Helen throughout and held his breath through many snide comments from her mother. He would get the last word tonight. He would put an end to the foolishness.

But suddenly he realized that he might have waited for too long. As the plates were being cleared and the men began to get up to go to the smoke room, he realized he had almost let his opportunity slip him by. It was now or never.

"Mr. and Mrs. Beckwith, thank you for having me for dinner." Karl found himself standing, which was a bit awkward, but he barreled on, too anxious to stop. *He could do this.*

"I want to thank you again for letting me join you here on the *Titanic* and spend time with Helen. I know it was a bit of a surprise to you and I thank you for your hospitality. I also want to thank you for the wonderful time I was able to spend with your family in Europe. It was a lovely vacation and I apologize once again for my absent-mindedness that may have given you the mistaken impression that I did not appreciate the honor. However, despite the glorious ten days of exotic travel, I feel as though we did not get a proper chance to know one another there, so I would like to tell you a few things about myself. I currently have two jobs, working both at a leading law firm on Wall Street and at my father's company, Herman Behr & Co. I graduated from Yale and have a law degree from Columbia. I also play tennis, as you know, having captained the Yale team and been ranked in the top ten in the United States five times. I've made the Wimbledon final in doubles and had the great honor of representing our country in the Davis Cup."

Mrs. Beckwith did not look impressed. Mr. Beckwith hung his head. A feeling of desperation flooded over him.

"More importantly, I love your daughter Helen very, very much. I'd like to think that over time I can win your approval, for I believe you will find it difficult to find a better match than me, Mrs. Beckwith. In fact, I do believe I am the perfect suitor for Helen, if you don't mind my saying, and....and.... well, I do not appreciate the way you have treated me these past few weeks."

His voice was too loud. He was painfully aware that he had gone off script. Other tables were staring. Perhaps, on second thought, he shouldn't have stood for his speech. Mrs. Beckwith just stared at him, bemused.

"Mr. Behr! That will be enough." Mrs. Beckwith was completely exasperated, not playing her part in his script at all.

For the first time since he leaped into his speech Karl glanced over at Helen, who looked about as meek as he had ever seen her. Deep down, he now realized, he had hoped she would jump up and come to his defense, fight for him the way that he was fighting for her.

Instead, he looked at her, locking eyes and for the first time feeling as if they were not in perfect harmony. She looked appalled, aghast, helpless.

His rush of adrenaline drained away like old bathwater. He realized that he was out on this limb alone. People at other tables were still looking.

Helen looked up at him. What did she want him to do now? There was, unfortunately, no way to go back in time two minutes. Well, at least he had stood up for himself, had put it all out there. If nothing else, they would know he was a man who was not to be treated in such a manner. There was no going back in time. What was he going to do?

He took one last look at the blank faces looking back at him and knew his plan had failed. He needed to get out of there. He excused himself and quickly walked out, afraid to look back.

After dinner that night, Harry dragged Dick and Jack away from the smoking room.

"Boys, I have a surprise for you! It is a very special night for you. Follow me." He led them through the ship's maze-like corridors.

"Where in heaven's name are we going, Harry?" Jack asked.

"It's a secret, just follow me."

Dick was confused, and a bit put off, when they ended up in Harry's suite.

"Harry, really, what are we doing here?" he asked, more than a little impatient at this point.

But Harry seemed not to be listening to them. He went over to the safe and started to unlock it. Dick and Jack looked at each other. Harry was a character, that was for sure.

"I've heard rumors about you having lots of money, no need to prove it to us!" Jack quipped, but Harry didn't even flinch. He opened the safe and stepped back so the boys could see. There were no wads of cash or stacks of gold, no fine watches or paintings – just about a dozen books.

"You keep books in there?" Jack exclaimed, seeming to be almost repulsed by the thought. But Dick was intrigued. He couldn't imagine this, a fellow who had access to the greatest riches, keeping books in a safe.

He watched Harry's excitement as he pulled the books, daintily as could be, out of the safe and laid them out on the bed as if any rash movement would ruin them.

"I told you I'd show you my books, Dick. Here they are."

Dick leaned over to touch one that caught his eye, but Harry stopped him.

"Sorry, no finger-prints. You have to put gloves on if you want to touch them. These are rare editions."

"Let's get back to the smoking room or the café," Jack whined. He looked to Dick but received no help there. "Well, I'll catch up with you fellows later." With an exasperated shrug, he left the room.

Dick was intrigued. Harry handed him a pair of gloves. Then he passed one particularly delicate-looking volume over to Dick, opening the pages.

"What is it?" He asked.

"It's a rare copy of *Bacon's Essays* written by Francis Bacon in *1598*," Harry said proudly.

"That's incredible," Dick said, gently flipping through the pages.

Harry nodded, clearly pleased by Dick's enthusiasm. "Yes it is."

Dick laid the tome down gently, fearful of damaging it. He was certain that Harry would never forgive him if he did, and

Harry Widener, the influential Harvard alum, was a person he wanted to have on his side.

"When you get to Cambridge I can show you around the campus if you'd like. You can see my collection in the library there – I've been working on it since my second year of graduate school. I can also introduce you to some professors. If you like, that is. I realize your father knows plenty of people too."

"He knows all the tennis affiliated people there. That's about it. I doubt he could name a single law professor. But tell me, Harry. How did you get involved in this biblio... whatever it is you called it."

"I was taking theatre classes at Harvard and while researching a paper I was discovered this quite old play in the stacks, hundreds of years old it seemed. I had never seen pages printed or colorized quite like that before. I talked to the librarian about it and I began to do research on the history of this book. What can I tell you? It just took over my whole life. I realized how many rare, classic books there must be just floating around without anyone taking care of them or even knowing they're there, important pieces of literature and history – stuff that should be preserved. I'm lucky that I had the means to do it. When I talked to my father about doing that as opposed to going into banking, he was supportive of the idea. And now I can't imagine doing anything else. You have to have passion, Dick. Life is pretty boring without it. And rare books are my passion."

Dick really didn't know what to say. He hadn't quite inherited his father's adroitness in conversation. But he did find something inspiring about Harry's story, as odd – and reeking of entitlement – as it was.

"What's your passion, Dick Williams?" Harry asked.

He didn't know what to say. Tennis, he supposed, though that was more his father's passion. And anyway, it was just a sport, nothing you could build a life around. That was the question. What was his passion?

"Well, I like history," he said. It was the truth and something that seemed to fit into the flow of conversation.

"Well, as I said, I know the history professors. There's a lot you can get involved in on campus."

"I'm afraid my schedule's going to be pretty full with tennis and tournaments though. Seems to be a priority for my father, peculiar as that may be. He doesn't want me doing too much outside of classes, so I can keep in shape."

The thought of how much tennis would take over his life once he got to America concerned Dick. He had tried to not think about it, but New York was only a few days away.

"Is that your passion? To just play tennis? To be a star athlete?" Harry asked.

"I am not certain Harry," said Dick.

That was the truth. He was not sure how he was going to feel when he arrived in the United States. He hoped that that he would be struck with a passion that Harry had that would lead him down a path to his life's pursuits. Tennis in the United States was an unknown to Dick and it was not a guarantee that it would be enjoyable or that he would be successful.

"There's no harm in that Dick. Just keep looking. You'll know when you find it."

Karl couldn't sleep that night. He just lay on top of his bed, fully clothed, second-guessing the entire evening. He was still a bit tipsy and he was angry at everything, unable to believe what had happened that night. Angry at himself for coming on this ship at all, for putting himself in such an untenable position, for getting so carried away that night. He was angry with Mrs. Beckwith for opposing him for no good reason. He was angry at everyone who had watched him make a fool out of himself without intervening. He was even angry at Helen for not standing up for him, for not running after him – and for making him fall in love with her in the first place. Now everything was hopeless.

He thought he heard a knock on the door. He listened more closely and there it was again. It was almost two in the morning. He couldn't imagine why anyone would be knocking on his door at that hour. Perhaps a crew member had his room confused with someone else. But when he heard the knock a third time he decided he'd better go check.

It was Helen. She seemed exasperated, standing there with her hair unbraided and cascading down her back, with only a light jacket covering her nightgown. She was panting and he could see that she had been crying. He knew he should do something, invite her in, hug her, say something, but he couldn't stop staring at her. She was so beautiful.

Luckily, she let herself in and closed the door behind her. She threw her jacket to the ground and without a word fell into his arms. They collapsed onto the bed together, undressing, kissing, touching.

He had made it clear to Helen early on in their courtship that she need not worry about any pressure of that sort from him. He was a traditional fellow and was willing to wait as long as she wanted. She was a virgin, he correctly assumed, and he had always believed that their first lovemaking would be on their wedding night.

Whether he'd known it or not, though, this was everything Karl had always wanted, though it was all happening at the wrong time in the wrong way. He should stop. He should talk to her and make sure she knew what she was doing, but she was the one leading the way, and in his slightly drunk and worked-up state, he struggled to get in control of the situation.

Her touch, her skin, her lips, her sturdy but delicate frame pressed against his, her assertiveness — it was all so wonderful, but he couldn't go through with it. Not like this, not after what had happened at dinner — not before he proposed.

The ring.

"Helen, wait," he said, pushing her off gently and standing up.

He looked at her lying there, in only her slip, looking so vulnerable and frightened.

"Did I do something wrong?" she said, a hint of anger in her voice.

"No, no, it's just that I thought we should talk first. Let's light a candle. I wanted it to be special."

"Funny man. You'd think I was the man and you were the girl," she scoffed, putting her nightgown in place and looking for her jacket.

"Wait, don't go, please." He went to the closet and searched for the jacket he'd been wearing at dinner – the ring was still in there. This was it, this was the moment, and he had to show her what his plans were.

"Karl, I'm sorry. I'll just see you tomorrow. This is embarrassing now." She turned her back and started walking towards the door.

"Wait, Helen!" he shouted, as he got down on one knee.

She turned around and saw him. He was hoping for a reaction like the stewardess gave her that day when he had so excitedly displayed the ring. Instead she just stared, silent, her expression unchanged. This was not how he had pictured it.

"Helen, I love you, will you marry me?" he finally said, hoping she was just waiting for him to say the words. Instead she remained silent and went over and sat on his bed, keeping her jacket on. He got up and went to sit next to her.

"Karl, what are we doing? We can't do this." She sounded resigned. He was crushed.

"Never?" he asked, confused. He thought she wanted to marry him too.

"No, but not like this. Not right now. With my mother still so angry and after what just happened. It's just not the right time." He knew she was right, but he still couldn't believe he was hearing those words. He put the ring back into his pocket.

"I'll see you tomorrow." She kissed him on the forehead and walked quietly out of the room, leaving him even more nonplussed than he'd been fifteen minutes before.

8

It had been a rather uneventful day. The air had been unusually cold, keeping most of the passengers indoors. Dick had taken advantage of that, putting on his fur coat and walking the empty decks with Harry and Jack. He had a lot to think about.

He thought back to the operetta he had seen the night before they boarded, *The Count of Luxembourg.* It was a love story about the twists and turns of society life. The Grand Duke is in love with a woman but his parents won't allow him to marry her because she has no title. So he pays a penniless count to marry and then divorce her, but the count is not allowed to see his arranged bride, even during the wedding ceremony. After the marriage, however, the two meet and fall in love, without even realizing they are already husband and wife. It was a story of how societal pressures can greatly influence the pursuit of happiness in one's life. Dick's circumstances were very different but he could intimately relate.

That evening, the Wideners hosted a special dinner for Captain Smith and he and his father were among a very special select group of invitees. The food at this dinner stood out even from the usual fine cuisine of the main dining room and included some of the most delicious Belgian hothouse grapes he had ever had. He indulged himself, not that overeating ever had much effect on him. He could always eat as much as he wanted and still feel thin and nimble on court in the morning.

After dinner, the usual group – Major Butt, John Thayer and William Dulles gathered in the smoking room for a nightcap. With the captain now absent, Mr. Thayer brought up a small concern. He and his wife had been talking with the captain earlier that day when a deck hand came to him with an iceberg warning they'd received over the wireless. Mrs. Thayer had been rather flustered by the news, although Captain Smith had assured her that there was no cause for concern.

"John, there is no need to worry," said Charles. "Even if an iceberg hit this ship, can you even imagine that it might sink?"

"They do call it the unsinkable ship," Major Butt echoed.

"I'm sure you're right," Mr. Thayer replied, though he didn't sound very confident.

"Look, John," said Charles, "Even if we did hit an iceberg, which we are not going to of course, there is no way in the world that this ship will sink. I've been on a ship that hit an iceberg before and we all survived." Dick sat up straight – he had never heard his father mention such a thing!

"You don't say Charles?" Mr. Dulles teased. "I suppose you merely steered the ship to safety yourself?"

Charles gave him a stern glare and leaned forward to tell the story.

"It was November of 1879. I was just about nineteen years old, just a couple of years younger than my son over there. The ship was the *Arizona*. I was accompanying my father on a business trip, already nearly running the family business myself of course. The ship was small, about a tenth of the size of this one I'd say. It was a cargo ship, carrying cotton down to St. John and my father was going to set up a labor shop down there, which was just about as illegal and as dangerous as you could get, but you had to break some rules to start such a business back in those days. My father, may he rest in peace, really relied on me."

"Well they didn't have these fancy alert systems and the wireless like they do now and sure enough, one exceptionally cold night, we hit an iceberg. After a brief moment of panic after impact, it was really no big deal at all. Everyone on board just started using the cotton in the cargo and stuffing the hole of the ship! It slowed us down a bit but that was all. And as I said, John, that boat was nothing compared to this."

The story captivated all of them and had certainly seemed to assuage the concern that Mr. Thayer had been feeling. Dick was particularly enthralled and surprised that he had never known this about his father. He tried to imagine what his father must have been like at his age and what his relationship with his own father had been like. Why had he never talked about this before?

Everyone was tired that night after the luxurious meal and they all retreated back to their rooms early. Dick walked with his father down the meandering corridors to their cabin on the D Deck, a familiar stroll already just a few nights into the voyage. The *Titanic,* in all its glory and grandeur, was beginning to feel like home.

"You've been awfully quiet today son," Charles said. "Anything on your mind?"

"I'm fine, Pops, just tired."

"I bet you're just nervous about your squash game tomorrow. Don't worry, you'll be fine. I wouldn't have set it up if I didn't know you were up to the challenge and in for a good time."

The day had dragged on forever. Karl spent most of it in his room sulking. He knew he should give Helen some space after everything they had been through the previous night – the dinner, Helen's advances, the failed proposal. It was a lot to take in and he thought some distance would do him good, but throughout the day things had only become more and more dire in his head. What if there was no way to fix everything? At the end of the day, he went up to the top deck and watched the sunset. The cold air seemed to highlight the peaches and purples in the sky. He found hope in the beauty. He wished that Helen was there with him, in his arms. But tomorrow would come and with it a new chance and yet another fresh start. If they were truly meant to be together, if love mattered at all, then it would all work out for the best. As the *Titanic* glided quickly through the water, he went to eat a steak dinner by himself, then had a drink in the smoking room until late. Eventually, he found himself strangely at peace.

Back in his room around eleven-thirty, he began to prepare for bed. He didn't sleep well at all after the drama of the night before, so he was looking forward to a full night of rest. He removed his collar, cutaway vest and coat when he suddenly was knocked a bit off balance. The ship had trembled slightly. Perhaps a shaft had broken? The engines were still running, so it couldn't be that. He put his vest back on and peaked out into the hallway, but it was empty and calm, so he went back into his room. However, as he took off the vest again he realized that the engines had indeed stopped.

He didn't know what was going on, but he knew that he wouldn't be able to go to sleep until he knew what had happened and knew that Helen was safe. He ran through the empty dining room and reception room to her cabin on the D Deck. Something was most certainly going on. Helen, the Beckwiths and the Kimballs were all gathered outside in the corridor.

"Karl!" Helen saw him and came running and they embraced. It felt so good to hold her. Mrs. Beckwith cleared her throat, but nobody else in the group seemed to pay her any mind.

"What's going on?" he asked.

"We hit an iceberg!" said Helen. "Karl, it broke Mother's window and actually stuck into her room!"

Karl looked over to Mr. Beckwith, who nodded in confirmation, pointing to the room where Mr. Kimball was standing next to a chunk of ice, inspecting it.

"Mr. Beckwith, we should go check out the rest of the ship and see if the crew know about your room."

"You're right, Karl," he said, sounding relieved to have some help. "I'll go down below with Edwin to see if we can find anything. Why don't you go survey the deck?"

"Yes sir." Karl nodded.

"I'm going with you," Helen proclaimed, putting her arm through his and holding on tight.

"All right then. Honey, you and Gertrude stay here in case anyone comes. Will you be okay?" Mr. Beckwith said to his wife, who looked visibly shaken.

"Mother, we'll be right back, I promise," Helen assured her.

"Everything is fine, I'm certain of it," said Mr. Beckwith. "We just want to get our facts straight and we'll all meet back here in ten minutes." He walked over to his wife and put his hand on the back of her neck, bringing her head to his chest and bending down to give her a kiss. It was the most intimate moment Karl had witnessed between the two. He felt Helen sink into him at the sight.

Karl led Helen, hand in hand, up onto the deck above. It was deserted. "It seems as if everything is okay," Helen said, so matter of factly. He wasn't sure if she was talking about the condition of the ship or their relationship, and he sincerely hoped she meant both. Knowing that he had to make the most of their moments alone, he grabbed her hands and pulled her towards him.

"Helen, I am so, so, sorry."

"Karl, don't..."

"No, Helen. Last night just went wrong, for so many reasons."

She interrupted him the best way she knew how, a move of desperation that always worked. She leaned in to kiss him, kissing him in such a passionate way that she knew he'd be out of breath for minutes to come.

"Karl, it's fine. Everything that happened. All of it...was my fault."

"Did your mother hear you come in last night?"

"I think so, but we didn't talk about it much today."

"Do you think she'll accept me?"

"Never," Helen joked and he pinched her on her sides in punishment. Everything was going to be fine.

He checked his watch, glancing around the empty deck again.

"We better get back and let them know that everything is fine up here."

The two walked hand in hand back to the stateroom and Karl was satisfied enough with the ship's solidity to get back into bed. But when they got back to the D Deck, the mood was still tense, with Mr. Beckwith and Mr. Kimball deep in discussion,

"What's the matter?" Karl asked.

"The squash courts are flooded," said Mr. Beckwith "It's up to the ankle down there."

"What does this mean Richard?" exclaimed Mrs. Beckwith from the bedroom.

Karl suddenly pictured the lifeboats he found himself leaning against earlier that evening. "I know where the lifeboats are," he said. "Perhaps we should go up there. If we're by the lifeboats we'll be the first to know if anything is seriously wrong."

Everyone seemed to agree this was a good idea. There was no real sense of urgency, just a desire to stay on top of the situation and make sure they put themselves in the best possible position in case anything did happen. They grabbed their coats and walked up the Grand Staircase. Captain Smith passed them going in the opposite direction, but he said nothing.

When they finally reached the upper deck, it was not nearly as empty as the other side had been a mere twenty minutes earlier. Despite the larger crowd, though, there was still no sense of panic. Some people still had on their nightgowns, with coats thrown over them. Others either still had on or had put back on their evening clothes. They were all tired, curious, just standing there waiting for some sort of direction, not wanting to go to sleep for fear that they would miss out on the excitement. A loud bang and hiss caused everyone to jump, but it was just the sound of the steam pipes continuing to do their job.

They were going to be fine.

He squeezed Helen's hand to make sure she knew it too.

⎯⎯ᴏ/ᴏ/ᴏ⎯⎯

A jolt woke Dick up from a deep sleep. He looked to his right and his father was sitting up in bed too, looking as disoriented as he himself felt. They both walked over to look out the porthole but the view was as beautiful as ever. Everything looked calm. The ship was still gliding through the Atlantic.

"What time is it?" Dick asked. Charles always had his pocket watch on him, even when sleeping.

"Eleven forty-five. Do you think we should go see what's going on? Do you hear anything?"

He listened intently to the noises on the ship. It was clear that the engines had been turned off, as the gentle and soothing throbbing sound they had grown so accustomed to was no longer there. Instead, there was a distinct hissing noise, likely from the steam pipes, and a slight grating sound. Nothing too alarming, but he was certainly curious.

"We should go check on things," Charles said with excitement, never wanting to miss out on a big event. He went to the closet and got out their fur coats, recalling how cold it had been earlier that night and imagining it would only be worse right now, especially after having been asleep.

They walked out to the hallway, which was almost empty, and he wondered if everyone else had slept through the jolt. The few people who were out there seemed calm, at the most a bit inquisitive.

As they rounded the corner, they heard the first sign of commotion. The door handle on a suite had been jammed and the occupant, clearly alarmed to have heard a collision and not be able to get out, was beginning to panic.

"Don't worry ma'am," a stewardess assured her. "I've called maintenance and they are on their way."

"Please, get me out of here now," the woman behind the door screamed, sounding frantic. Dick decided to take action.

"Excuse me. Ma'am," he called. "Take a step back from the door. I'm going to knock it down!"

"Thank you! I'm clear," the muffled voice replied.

"Sir, you can't do that," the stewardess intervened. Dick locked eyes with his father and with a grin on his face rammed his shoulder into the door, jolting it wide open. He was greeted with a hug and a kiss on the cheek by the lady inside and he and his father continued on up to the deck. The stewardess shouted after them, "Sir, I will be forced to report you for having damaged official White Star property!"

He and his father rushed towards the stairwell. Charles put his hand on his shoulder and they laughed as they made their way up to the deck on the starboard side. They were a bit startled to find the deck fairly empty and calm. The cold air seemed to be keeping people down below. There was an eerie silence since the engines weren't running but the ship was still gliding through the water. Soon a few more people joined them on deck in various stages of dress. There were rumors spreading that the ship had hit an iceberg.

They heard a commotion on the deck below and peered over the railing to see what was happening. A few teenagers had gathered some ice in a bucket and were proudly displaying it and tossing pieces at one another.

"Look at that, Pops! We must have actually hit something."

Charles glared at the bucket of ice intently. Dick searched the lines on his father's face for any sign of worry. If there was no outer damage to the ship, then the iceberg must have hit below decks, which was not good. Still, the ship was "unsinkable."

"My boy, it looks like we'd better go find some cotton!" Charles said with a grin.

9

Karl stood on the deck, his arms around Helen to make sure she stayed warm.

Distress rockets were fired, filling the sky with beautiful fireworks. It would have been so romantic if indeed fireworks were what they were. Still, the people on deck remained calm as a few officers came out and began unleashing the lifeboats.

"Women and children only," they announced politely.

Mr. Beckwith and Mr. Kimball came up to the deck with armloads of life vests. As they all struggled to get them on, they watched as the first few brave passengers loaded into a lifeboat. It was a sixty-foot drop to the water and for the moment it seemed scarier to be lowered on the lifeboat than to stay on the sturdy ship. Even while watching the lifeboats load, it was impossible to imagine that anything bad could happen to this enormous ship. The first lifeboat departed only about a quarter full and even then the crew members struggled to lower it into the sea properly.

The managing director of the White Star Line, Bruce Ismay, came out to supervise the lifeboat process. That was when Karl realized how serious this was. He stayed calm and kept his fears to himself, but he had seen the damage himself. He had seen the ice come into the ship. He knew that they should not lose the opportunity to get Helen, Mrs. Beckwith and Mrs. Kimball off safely before anything got worse. The women had to be taken care of.

Of course, the last thing he wanted to do was be separated from Helen. It seemed their entire relationship had been a repeating chorus of being pulled together and pulled back apart. Now that they had connected in such an intimate way, now that he was standing here holding her right in front of Mrs. Beckwith without the slightest self-consciousness, feeling perfectly natural, it felt especially cruel that they would be torn apart.

Directly in front of them the officers were helping prepare another lifeboat to be lowered. Mr. Ismay approached their group.

"Mrs. Beckwith, I do hope you will climb aboard the lifeboat. We will send one of our best crewmen with you to make sure it goes smoothly."

"You should go, Sallie." Richard encouraged. Mrs. Beckwith gave him a kiss on the cheek and got onto the boat without arguing. She seemed to understand what was going on. Mrs. Kimball followed. All eyes were on Helen, who tightened her grip around Karl's waist.

"It's okay mother, I'm just going to wait for the next lifeboat with Karl."

"Helen, please," Mrs. Beckwith said sternly, gesturing at Karl to do something.

Karl looked her directly in the eyes and said as calmly as possible, "I'll be fine. I'll be down soon or you will be right back up, but right now they're only letting women on and you should really go to keep an eye on your mother."

"But I want to be with you," Helen whispered into his ear, tears beginning to form in her eyes.

"Helen, you're always with me. And I'm always with you. Just do this for me."

Helen nodded solemnly. She moved closer for one last kiss before turning around and letting Mr. Beckwith and a White Star officer, Herbert John Pitman, help her into the boat. It was still only about a third full.

"Is there anyone else for this boat? Any other women or children?" The officer called out. No one answered. There were no other women or children to be seen. Helen sat next to her mother and wept into her shoulder. Mrs. Beckwith looked up at her husband and Karl, side by side.

"Mr. Ismay, may the men come with us?" she asked quietly.

There was a pause as the director surveyed the barren deck.

"Of course, Madam, every one of you."

Karl was hesitant to join. He looked around the deck to make sure there were no women or children left. But when he looked into Helen's tear-filled eyes, he knew there was no way he could let her go without him.

"You can help with the rowing," the officer assured him.

With that he stepped off of the deck of the *Titanic* and into the lifeboat. He made his way carefully to Helen's side. Mr. Beckwith came in as well. A few other men heard the news and came running to be with their wives. It was very dark in the boat and hard to tell who was there and who wasn't, but they were already at half capacity and it would be difficult to lower all the way. The crew began lowering the boat.

"Is Edwin here?" Mrs. Kimball exclaimed, suddenly realizing that he hadn't come aboard. "Edwin!" she cried out. They were just below deck level. Suddenly his head popped over the railing and he rolled himself overboard. He rocked the boat considerably, but he made it. Another man, Dr. Henry Frauenthal, jumped in to join them. Frauenthal was so large that he needed two life vests. He landed on one of the female passengers, Mrs. Annie May Stengel, knocking her unconscious.

The descent was rough. The lifeboat kept swinging at sharp angles.

"Oh Karl!" Helen cried. "We're going to be swamped the second we get to the water if we don't steady!" She was right, but he didn't want her to know he agreed, so he just squeezed her hand.

"Officer Pitman, have you got the plug in the boat?" came a call from up on the deck.

"I think so," Pitman yelled back up, before making eye contact with Karl. "Mr. Behr, will you feel below you to make sure the plug is in?" Karl felt down but didn't know what he was looking for.

"It's your job to make sure that's in the boat, Officer Pitman!"

"I feel it. It's here!" Karl yelled back, relieved.

"Officer Pitman, you stay in the boat to help charge it. Watch after the others. Stand by to come back after the gangway is hailed!" They were almost to the water and had finally evened out.

"Yes sir, Officer Murdoch!" Officer Pitman yelled back.

"Good-bye. Good luck," came the final call from above.

When the boat finally made it to the water they were eye level with the D Deck portholes, the very deck they had been on a little over an hour ago.

"Does anyone have a knife?" Officer Pitman asked the passengers when they reached the sea. *This is not a good sign*, thought Karl. The men all searched their coat pockets and finally, after another great struggle, the ropes were cut. They were floating free of the *Titanic*.

Dick and Charles went back to their rooms to put their life vests on. Remembering the cold, they put their fur coats back on over them. It might be a long night and they wanted to be out on the deck to watch all of it. Dick was a little bit alarmed, but Charles continued to be amused by the whole series of events, relishing the thought of this being a new story to tell once they got to America.

"The boys aren't going to believe all of this ruckus," he remarked as they walked back on deck. "We didn't even have life vests on the *Arizona*."

"We might not have any cotton either," Dick joked, trying to make himself feel calmer.

"Guess not," Charles laughed.

When they got back to the starboard deck there was a procession of cooks and stewards bringing up loaves of bread, followed closely by mailmen carrying bags of mail.

"For the lifeboats," Charles said matter-of-factly. "Oh my, Richard, this will make all the papers. Your uncle is not going to believe it."

Sure enough, as Dick looked around, he could see that there were some crew members calmly unleashing the lifeboats and a few people gathered around them waiting to get in. The deck was a little more crowded than it had been earlier, but it was still mainly just people standing around calmly in life vests, wondering what was going on.

"This lifeboat is ready to be loaded," an officer announced. "Women and children only. Women and children only."

"Hmm. I've never seen them actually load a lifeboat before, son," Charles said.

"Are you sure everything is okay, Pops?" He couldn't help feeling worried. For the first time he sensed some nervousness in his father.

"Absolutely. This ship will not sink. I think the worst case scenario is that we'll float hobbled for a while and in the morning we'll all be loaded onto another ship."

It sounded reasonable. They leaned against the railing and watched as the crewmen loaded the lifeboat. When it was about halfway full there were no more women and children around, so they began to lower it. They were having quite a difficult time of it, so Dick went over to help. The boats were heavy and it was a far drop to the waterline. He hated to think what would happen if the lifeboats were full – it would have been impossible to get them down safely. There were a few emotional moments as wives and children separated from their husbands and fathers, but other than that the most dramatic part was the lowering itself.

Dick saw his father shivering and suggested that they go get some brandy to stay warm. It looked to be a long and suspenseful night. It was just after midnight and as they approached the bar they could see it was empty and the doors were locked. The bartender was there still sorting through his things but he wouldn't open the doors for them.

"I'm sorry," he said through the window. "The ship won't allow me to serve alcohol past midnight."

Charles was not amused. "You'd think they'd make an exception when the lifeboats are being loaded, for heaven's sake."

Charles took a flask out of his pocket, a beautiful silver one with a brown tortoiseshell cover, and slipped it into the inside pocket of Dick's fur coat.

"Not that it'll do you any good tonight, by the looks of it. But you should have this now. It should be yours." Dick felt a shiver as he took the flask. What about his father's irrepressible optimism? What about "This ship won't sink" attitude? And what good was it transferring the flask now? They were "in the same boat," so to speak. But he didn't say a word and just silently accepted the flask.

In an attempt to stay warm, they wandered back to the smoking room, where they ran into Mr. Thayer, Mr. Widener and Harry. The men shared a smoke, none betraying any concern about the night's events, each maintaining their calm and dignity, even Mr. Thayer, who had been so worried earlier in the evening.

"Well Dick, it looks like you're in luck," Mr. Thayer said with a pale smile. "I do imagine this will cancel our squash match."

"I sure got off easy there," said Dick. The iceberg had punctured the competitive bubble. "I'll have a few more days to practice." He did his best to mimic the forced bonhomie of those around him.

"I don't know where Jack wandered off to, Dick. Maybe you and Harry should go find him. He wandered away after we got Mrs. Thayer into a lifeboat."

Dick looked at his father. There was no way he was going to leave his side.

"I think I'll stay here, if that's okay with you, Mr. Thayer. Or perhaps we should all go find Jack together?" But Mr. Thayer didn't look like he was going anywhere and Dick didn't really want to either. It was a big ship and they could easily get separated on a night like this. Jack would be okay, he guessed.

"I see a ship! We're being rescued," a man yelled from the hallway.

"See son, what did I tell you?" Charles said. The men made their way out to the upper decks.

10

Dick beat the rest of the men racing out to the starboard deck, only to find that the lights the man was shouting about had been there all night and clearly weren't moving any closer. As the other men joined him and they looked around it became harder and harder to convince themselves that there was nothing serious going on. The ship was clearly listing and they were at least a deck closer to the water than they had been before.

Major Butt was there helping maintain order as the last of the lifeboats were lowered. Most people were calm, but there were definitely some who were panicking. Women sobbed. Some men went running back to their rooms to gather their wallets and jewelry from the safes, even throwing them onto lifeboats so they would be saved.

"I've got to go back and get my books," said Harry. "They'll be ruined!"

"We can't be like these men putting their jewels above human life," said Dick. "I know you love your books, but if the ship *does* go down, we've got to save ourselves and our fellow passengers. There won't be room for your library in the lifeboat."

"Stay with us, son. Please," Harry's father pleaded.

Finally the last of the lifeboats was cut free from the ship. That was it. Some rather adventurous men made a scene by attempting to jump from the deck into the lifeboats after realizing that there were no more ways of escaping the ship.

Dick could even swear he heard gunshots off in the distance, though it could have just been another call of distress being sent up by the ship. His group was fairly silent and calm. There wasn't much to say. It was as if they were merely observing a tragedy that was happening to others.

For the most part, in fact, there was still a sense of calm throughout the ship. The lights were still on and it all looked beautiful. The band played on, just as it would have in one of the operas that Dick loved so much. The men slowly walked the deck of the boat in silence. They leaned over the railing and watched the lifeboats gradually shrink with distance. They passed by the board that marked the daily runs. It felt like it was another lifetime when they had stared at that board, arguing over the arrival time in New York. No one had placed a bet that the ship wouldn't arrive at all.

"It might be a long night friends. Shall we?" Mr. Thayer gestured to the gym behind him, which McCawley had opened up for people to come in and stay warm on this strange, cold night. It was packed, and almost all of the bikes and rowing stations were being used. Mostly men were in there, but there were a few women scattered about who apparently had seen no reason to be separated from their husbands.

An exercise bike opened up and Dick wanted to make sure that his father got on. He knew with his fragile health that it was important for his father to stay warm and keep up his heart rate, especially if they were going to be out there for some time. He was overcome with a desire to protect his father, to shield him from everything that was happening. Charles's unwavering optimism, which sometimes annoyed Dick, now seemed like something he wanted to coddle and protect, like a sacred artifact. Harry wanted to protect his books. Other men wanted to protect their valuables, but Dick just wanted to protect his father.

Charles got on the exercise bike without putting up a fight at all. It was difficult with the slant of the boat, but he managed.

"I guess icebergs are good for business!" he yelled across the room to McCawley, who was running around trying to accommodate everyone.

"Sure is, Charlie, I should have thought of this years ago," he joked.

"Suction!" Officer Pitman kept yelling. "Suction!"

Out in the Atlantic, Karl and the others in Lifeboat 5 were trying to get as far away from the *Titanic* as possible, just in case the unthinkable happened. Of course, the unthinkable already was happening. They were living it, but still his mind couldn't take the next step. Loading the lifeboats seemed like such an extreme measure to begin with, an unnecessary precaution merely taken to appease the rule book. But as they continued rowing farther away from the ship, it was harder and harder to deny what was happening. And as Officer Pitman explained, one of the greatest dangers facing them now was being caught too close to the sinking ship and sucked under by the resulting rush of water. They needed to get as far away, as quickly as possible.

"Frank! Frank!" Mrs. Warren cried out repeatedly for her husband. In the darkness she hadn't realized until it was too late that Mr. Warren did not join them on the lifeboat.

Mrs. Beckwith tried to calm her down, stroking her hair and letting the woman cry in her lap.

Mrs. Kimball was the most fragile of their group and Mr. Kimball was showing a tenderness that Karl hadn't seen in him before, keeping her calm and warm. Helen sat completely stoic, her leg gently touching Karl's but otherwise keeping her hands to herself, trying to stay warm, trying to stay calm, trying to be patient.

Karl just kept rowing. The exercise kept him warm and the rhythm of the strokes helped in some ways to drown out the thoughts racing through his mind. Such as the fact that for the first time all trip he was without the ring. He left it behind in his room, not thinking to grab it when he ran to check on Helen. Of course, he could not have fathomed at the time that he would end up in a lifeboat, rowing away from the ship for fear of suction. There was no predicting this.

He thought of all the people left on the ship and hoped that all the women and children were able to find their way into the lifeboats. Their own was only about half full, so it seemed unlikely that there had been any problems. He was so glad to be with Helen, to be with her family, but he couldn't help but wonder if he should have stayed back to assist, to help others find their way.

He just kept rowing. He was afraid to look at scene unfolding back on the ship.

He heard Helen gasp and as he looked over to her he followed her eyes to where the *Titanic* was. Karl had been resisting the urge to look up and never could have imagined the sight he was now looking at. The ship was still completely lit up but only three decks were above water and those that were listed at a horrifying diagonal to the water. When they were all silent, he could still hear the orchestra playing.

Helen grabbed Karl's arm and began to sob.

Dick, Charles, Mr. Thayer and the Wideners didn't stay in the gym for long. Hearing more and more commotion outside, they left as soon as it seemed Charles was warm again. Walking back onto the deck of the ship was like walking through a time warp. The sporadic signs of chaos they witnessed earlier escalated exponentially in the few minutes they were in the gym.

There were only two decks of the ship above water now and the slant of the deck had intensified. All around them men began to jump off the ship and women and children who were unable to get off were sobbing. The orchestra played on calmly, eerily, and the lights were still working, but these were practically the only signs that this was the same ship they had been on earlier in the evening.

The highest point of the ship now was the captain's bridge, and having visited there earlier that evening to escort Captain Smith to dinner, Mr. Widener led the group there. Captain Smith and a quartermaster stood there, stoically observing the White Star liner disappear into the sea. From the lookout they had a clear view of the chaos on board as everyone scrambled to the starboard side, which was higher. No words were spoken, but as they began to feel the ship plummet faster the captain looked over to the men and nodded. They knew it was time to each go their own way.

Dick and Charles walked away from the bridge, sticking close with their friends, feeling somehow safer in numbers, still trying to assimilate what was happening. The *Titanic* was going to sink.

Suddenly the ship lurched and when Dick looked behind him, his friends were no longer there. They washed away into the frigid ocean. There was only water and a mast sticking out where the ship had been. Before he could grasp what was happening, icy water came rushing over him and instinct took control of his body.

He remembered the starboard rail that had been right in front of him and thought of the suction that they had been warned about. He swam with all of his might to the railing. As he swam, the ship came back under him and for an instant he found his footing again. He looked around frantically for his father and friends. He didn't see the Wideners or Mr. Thayer, but there, only about twelve feet from him stood his father. Holding onto the railing to keep his balance he ran towards him, knowing that their dry footing was temporary and that they had to keep moving.

"Get to the railing, Pops! We have to jump quickly!" He yelled the commands to his father, who ran with all his might towards the railing, but it was too late.

The ship lurched again and this time began to plummet like a toy dropped from a child's hands. He heard a loud snap and one of the four gigantic smokestacks that they had been standing near, the ones he had marveled at the day they arrived, came crashing down directly onto his father.

He stood still for a moment, transfixed by the steam still coming out of the collapsed pipe.

His father was gone.

Without an opportunity to digest what had just happened, he found that he was moments away from being again being pushed into the sea as the ship plunged farther into the deep. He knew he had to jump as far away from the ship as possible to save himself. He climbed on top of the railing, held his breath and leaped as far out as he possibly could.

The impact of the freezing water nearly knocked the breath completely out of him. But even underwater he kept thinking about the suction of the ship as it went under and knew he had to get as far away from the ship as possible. He finally reached the surface and knew the first thing he must do was get rid of his shoes and his fur coat. His shoes came off easily but the fur coat that had provided so much comfort earlier in the night now was more like a straitjacket. Unable to get it off, he twisted himself around so he was facing the ship again. He was certain he wasn't far enough away yet to avoid being pulled under in the suction and as he looked up he saw the three propellers of the ship high above his head, perfectly and beautifully lit up against the night sky. He had to get out of his coat and keep swimming or else they would certainly be the last thing he ever saw.

And then, as he watched helplessly, the ship, like a doomed dancer, performed a semicircle rotation and disappeared completely into the Atlantic Ocean. It happened so suddenly and smoothly that Dick was unable to get any farther away, but the ship vanished without so much as a wave or a hint of suction.

Dick was surrounded by the cries of hundreds of people in his predicament. They bobbed in their life vests, paralyzed by the freezing cold water, struggling to stay afloat. Out of the corner of his eye he thought he saw a black dog treading water. He wondered if it could be Mr. Dulles's prize bulldog, but he didn't have time to dwell. He knew his only shot of survival was to get away from the crowd and find something to float on.

Far off in the distance he saw a group of people climbing up onto a floating object. He swam as quickly as he could, still unable to wrangle off his soaking wet fur coat. As he approached the object, he realized it was a collapsible lifeboat and that there were a lot more people around it than he had originally realized, all struggling to get on. He figured if he could swim around and come at it from another angle he would have a better shot at getting on.

Maybe those last few days of working out in the gym would prove more valuable than just helping him win a squash match. He felt his years of athletic training, both physical and mental, as a lifesaving asset. In a burst of strength, he was able to ignore the cold for a few extra moments and swim around and claim his spot on the collapsible. Here it was, a chance for survival. The lifeboat had been swamped before the sides had been erected, so it was now no more than a platform without sides. Those clinging to it had the option of balancing on it and standing for a few moments waist deep in water, or holding on from the side. It wasn't ideal, and it didn't offer any permanent respite from the bone-chilling water, but it was better than nothing. In fact, it was the difference between life and death. It also allowed him, at last, the freedom to finally take off his elegant, saturated, albatross of a fur coat.

11

The *Titanic* was gone.

Karl squeezed Helen's hand. A tear streamed down his face. The horizon was now empty.

An unbearable chorus of cries arose from the ocean. They had just watched all those people plummet into the water. The cold, cold water.

Officer Pitman took out his pocket watch and noted that the time of the sinking was 2:20 a.m.

"Perhaps we should pray." Mr. Kimball offered.

They put down the paddles, held each other's freezing cold hands and said the Lord's Prayer. They could hardly hear themselves over the cries.

There was no way to tell how many people were stranded in the seas without a lifeboat, but as long as there were cries there were people that were alive. Karl looked at all the room available on their boat and couldn't help but wonder how many they could save.

"Perhaps, Officer Pitman, perhaps we should go back and fill up our boat?" Karl suggested softly.

"Heavens, Karl, we would be swamped in an instant," the hysterical Mrs. Kimball snapped. Though everyone else was silent, he surveyed the faces of those in his lifeboat and everyone seemed to agree. Helen just clung to Karl's shoulder, too cold to speak. He locked eyes with Mrs. Beckwith, who just gave him a nod.

"We would be swamped. We would all be dead!" Mrs. Kimball continued.

"I'm afraid she's right. It's too dangerous," Officer Pitman said.

———✧✧✧———

It's cold. My legs hurt. It's really cold. Are we going to survive? Am I going to make it? Holy God, it's cold.

These were pretty much the only thoughts running through Dick's brain as he slowly froze to death. It was impossible for his mind to assimilate the events of the evening. It didn't seem like understanding right now would do him any good. He knew he had to keep his limbs moving. He had to stay awake and keep his mind alert. He had heard the distress signals sent up. Surely someone was on their way to rescue them. He just had to hold on and he knew he could hold on better than anyone.

Throughout the night there were fifteen to twenty people on board the collapsible. Occasionally a wave would come by and force them to squat and hold onto submerged seats with their numb hands. But they were clearly the lucky ones. It didn't take very long for the cries from the open water to die down. Without anything to hold onto, those left in the water to fend for themselves were quite literally freezing to death. Dick wished to God they didn't have the life vests on. Drowning would have been more humane. He was glad his father hadn't suffered that fate.

The darkness was so total now that it was impossible to make out the faces of those on the collapsible with him, but they kept alert by talking to one another. They talked about when a ship would come. They counted off to pass the time. They occasionally sang songs and said prayers. Most of these orations faded away before they were finished, but finishing them wasn't the point.

There was no way to tell how much time was passing or whether the end of their suffering was in sight. All they could do was hold on and hope. Dick kept focus on those around him, observing just as he always did. He noticed that the man next to him barely fit into his life vest. He was jealous at first as he was sure that the man's natural padding would help keep him warmer than the rest. But after a while he felt the man collapse on his shoulder and realized he was dead. Dick gently pushed him off, peeled his hands off the boat and let him silently float away.

He became fixated on a dent on the top hat of the man in front of him. It seemed absurd to have such an elegant hat on under these circumstances at all. How in the world had he managed to swim all of this way with it still on? But perhaps this man was smart, surely it was helping his head stay warm. Dick just could not get over his urge to reach out and pop the dent out. He tried in four different languages to tell this man about the dent, certain that the second he realized what was wrong he would jump at the chance to fix it. But the man didn't understand him, or couldn't hear him, or just didn't care. Finally, overcome with a sense of urgency about fixing this dent right here and now Dick reached his hand out, but the man smacked it away violently with a shout of "No!" that nearly knocked them both off of the collapsible.

The cries grew softer and softer. The night, already pitch black, seemed to grow even darker.

The bottom of Karl's lifeboat had a leak in it. At first he thought that he had been wrong and that they had actually left the plug on the ship, but that wasn't the case. The boat itself was simply leaking. Helen was trying to hide the fact, but she was shaking with cold. Karl let Mr. Beckwith take over the rowing and he focused his energy on keeping Helen warm.

As the night wore on and hope seemed farther and farther away, more a dream than a reality, a handsome gentleman dressed in his evening clothes sitting next to Karl discreetly nudged him and revealed a small nickel-plated revolver. "Should worse come to worst you may use this revolver for your wife and yourself, after my wife and I have finished with it." There was no panic to his voice, no sense of desperation. Karl, horrified, just thanked him and continued rubbing Helen's feet.

Though it was a beautiful night inundated with stars, they provided little respite from the pitch-black night. Nobody on board Karl's boat had a light, and combined with the cold and the hunger, it became difficult for them all to grasp what was going on around them. As unbearable and frightening as the darkness was, it also in many ways provided a security blanket. Karl could hold on tight to Helen, feel her warmth and close his eyes to the rest of the tragedy. Mrs. Beckwith kept expressing her impatience for the sun to come up, clearly hoping it would help with the rescue and her coldness, but a part of Karl was afraid for a new day to begin, afraid to see what this tragedy had wrought. For the time being, he could hold onto Helen and pretend it was a dream they were all going to wake up from.

Any time a light was spotted, there was a stirring in the lifeboat. It very much reminded Karl of when he was riding out from the port at Cherbourg on the *Nomadic*, when everyone on the ferry would jump in anticipation anytime a ship was spotted, hoping it would be the great *Titanic*, the ship of dreams. But just like those false sightings the other day – could it possibly be just the other day? – the lights in the distance now ended up as disappointments, just someone's light on another lifeboat. This time the consequences were much greater, though. The night wore on and the cold got worse. Karl was startled when the man next to him offered his gun, but now he couldn't help but fight off the possibility that it could soon come to that.

Just when all hope seemed to be lost, when it seemed they had been floating there, rowing in circles to keep warm, for an infinite amount of time, when he wondered if this was actually a nightmare, an experience he *could* wake up from, he noticed the ocean beside him begin to sparkle. He looked around, certain the sun must be coming up, bracing himself for what laid ahead.

But there was no sun on the horizon. Rather, the sky seemed to be glowing behind the blanket of darkness, with streaks of light running through it, causing the sea to glimmer. It was the most spectacular sight Karl had ever seen.

"The Northern Lights," Mr. Beckwith said. "I've never seen them before."

The irony was not lost on any of them. Here, in the midst of the greatest tragedy any of them could have ever conceived being a part of, they were seeing one of the most wondrous sights possible in nature. Karl didn't know whether it was a sign of hope, a cruel joke, or just another thing too overwhelming to comprehend.

Eventually another lifeboat pulled up next to them. Officer Pitman ordered that they tie the two boats together so they could spread out and Helen could move away from the leak. The boat they tied to was even emptier than their own. There couldn't have been more twenty people on board. Karl feared to look at the faces, thankful to the dark for keeping everyone in hiding. He didn't want to see what this night had done to those around him. He focused on keeping Helen warm, but he could not get the feeling out of his head that he had failed his responsibility as a human being. He knew the danger had been real if they had tried to pick up loose survivors. There was a chance they would have been overwhelmed and the lifeboat would have sunk. But he was far from certain that it wasn't worth the risk.

And then, the guilt of the survivor was beginning to mount. He was only on that lifeboat because of Helen and Mrs. Beckwith. If he hadn't run to check on Helen despite thinking that everything was fine that evening, if Mrs. Beckwith hadn't asked if he could come on board, he wouldn't be here. It seemed unfair to all the men left on the *Titanic*. It seemed impossible that these lifeboats were so empty when so many had not been able to board, so many were left to die. Karl couldn't help keeping a running tally of every steward, friend, person he saw on that ship, and just kept saying prayers for all of them. He should have stayed back. He should have stayed to help.

None of this should have happened. There should not be a black hole of space where the greatest ship in the world had just been floating. They should not have hit an iceberg, should not have been transformed from elegant, privileged ocean liner passengers into ragged, freezing survivors in lifeboats.

It was all absolutely wrong. He listened to the sobs of the women around him who had not been lucky or bold enough to get their husbands on the lifeboats with them. He listened to the silence where cries had been coming from the water. He listened to the clanking of the paddles and the chattering of teeth, the heavy breathing and guilty and helpless silence in which they sat. He listened to it all, but it did not make sense. None of it made sense. None of it should be happening. He would trade everything he prized most – Sallie's approval, Helen's love – he would trade it all in for the world to make a bit of sense again. He was finally holding Helen close, in full view of the world, but this was not how it was supposed to happen.

Now the sun was rising and again Karl wished that it wouldn't. He did want to see the remains of the tragedy, to be given proof that what had happened was real. It was almost better in the dark.

But he knew that even in the comfort of the lifeboats they could not last much longer. That even with coats on and their upper bodies dry it was too cold to survive. They needed daylight to be seen.

"Karl, what's that over there?"

He looked over to where Helen was looking. Like a dream, like a vision, there was a ship. A big ship. A ship that was headed their way. He squeezed Helen's hand and she looked up to him with a gleam in her eye.

"Well I'll be," said Mrs. Beckwith in a breath of wonder.

There was no denying it this time. With the sun angling in from the horizon, and the mountains of icebergs all around them beginning to glisten, a ship was actually speeding towards them. It fired rockets just to confirm. He had never been more grateful for anything in his life. They were going to survive.

"Let's count again."

One... two...three...

The numbers coming out of their mouths didn't even make sense anymore. Dick wasn't even sure if they were correct. But every few minutes, or possibly hours – it was impossible to tell the difference anymore – someone would suggest they count off. It was mindless, but it kept them somewhat alert. It was comforting to hear voices and to attempt to use his own. Any sign of life in this situation, any positive group effort, no matter how trivial, was something to cling to.

They never finished counting, though. It was impossible to focus on anything long enough. Usually by the number six nobody on the collapsible could remember why they were counting or what number came next or whose turn it was. It didn't matter, Dick knew. The only thing that mattered was that they were still alive when they started the next round.

Dick was becoming more cold and exhausted as the moments passed and he could only assume that the others in his lifeboat were feeling the same way. He felt so close to those around him, to those holding on to the same hopes he was, but he resisted his usual urge to observe them. Looking too close at them now was too painful, too gut-wrenching. None of them stood a great chance to make it through the night. It was best not to get too intimate. He noticed the dents in top hats, kept silently recounting the number of people in the collapsible, but looked no farther than that.

Instead he looked deep within himself, something he wasn't used to doing. Many times throughout the night he thought about how nice it would be to go to sleep, to just close his eyes and let his body and mind float away from the cold and the horror of the situation. But he held on. His father did not have the chance to survive. The odds were not in favor for Mr. Thayer or the Wideners either. So he held on for them. His mother would be faced with a future without her husband and he had to be there to help her through that. He held on for her. Thomas McCawley, the gym attendant who had two children, had stayed at his post until the bitter end. He held on for him. He held on for the man next to him who had died on his shoulder earlier that night, for his friends whose fates he did not know yet. He felt he owed it to all of them to hold on.

But he also held on for himself. He wanted to go to America, to live with his uncle, to go to Harvard, and to find what the future held. He wanted to fight for his country as Major Butt had suggested. He wanted to study, to find his passion like Harry had encouraged. He wanted to meet new people and to fall in love. He wanted a chance to live his life. So he held on.

12

Captain Arthur Rostron of RMS *Carpathia* was interrupted from his sleep at 12:30 a.m. by his first officer H.V. Dean and wireless operator Harold Cottom. Cottom, who had stayed at his post late that night, had received a "CQD" distress signal that the *Titanic* had hit an iceberg. Captain Rostron immediately sprung from his bed, got dressed, checked the coordinates and redirected his ship full speed ahead towards the scene of the calamity. They were fifty-eight miles away and it would take almost four hours to get there. The *Carpathia's* full speed was usually 14½ knots, but to make it in time they ran at maximum speed of 17 ½ knots – a speed the ship had never seen before. The extra speed caused the ship to shake a bit, which woke up some of his passengers. Not knowing what was awaiting them when they got there he wanted to be as prepared as possible. He woke up all crew members and had them prepare all vacant rooms and public areas to accommodate survivors. He ordered a hot breakfast and coffee for them as well, had safety lights put on the side of the ship and had the crew prepare the ladder, ropes, canvas bags and slings to aid in rescuing passengers from lifeboats. He prepared the medical staff for the worst – the English doctor was asked to set up in the first-class dining room, the Italian doctor in the second-class dining room and the Hungarian doctor in the third-class dining-room. They were instructed to be ready with all supplies necessary for any emergency.

In Lifeboats 5 and 7, still tied together, Karl and the others watched breathlessly as the far-off light and rockets slowly approached. Dr. Frauenthal insisted that this ship wasn't coming for them – he had overheard an officer say that the only other ship nearby was the *Californian,* which wouldn't be there until the afternoon – but Karl clung to hope. It was all he had. He didn't know if they could make it to afternoon.

For the most part they sat shivering in silence. Three hours in the freezing cold Atlantic had taken its toll on all of them, though none would admit it. They were the lucky ones.

The water was calm. Karl focused on warming up Helen's feet. Mrs. Beckwith and Mrs. Kimball comforted Mrs. Warren. The men took turns rowing. Every once in a while someone would think to check on Mrs. Stengel, who was still passed out. What would she think when she woke up, he wondered? None of them had imagined this when they got into the lifeboats. Everything had been so calm.

The Northern Lights disappeared and dawn began to break. The light of the ship came closer and the hazy peach sky revealed the outline of a ship, her one funnel blowing puffs of smoke into the sky. He thought about the sunset he had seen just the night before and how much hope and comfort he had received from the colors of the sky. As different as things were now, the colors still signaled hope. They still provided comfort.

Carpathia stopped nearby, next to another lifeboat, and they could see and hear the commotion as the rescue began. There was an audible sigh in the boat as everyone sat up straight and stretched their freezing limbs, beginning to prepare for what lay ahead. They had done it. They were going to live.

They were next. Once again they ended up in the right place at the right time. The second boat in the water and the second boat out of the water. None of it made any sense. As the ship pulled up beside them, he studied the faces of those around him. Nobody cheered. Nobody said anything. They just focused on the task ahead.

A "Jacob's Ladder" was thrown down the side of the ship and a crew member scurried down to help them. This ship seemed so small compared to the leviathan they had been traveling on, but small was good. Small was safe. He squeezed Helen and she looked up at him and smiled, her face swollen from tears.

"Are there any children in your boat?" A voice shouted from above.

"No Sir! One injured though!" Officer Pitman yelled back.

"Good morning, folks. We have slings to help you on board if you need assistance. Otherwise if there are any women who feel healthy enough to climb on board we can begin that now."

"I will go first," Mrs. Beckwith said enthusiastically, leading the way for the women. It was quite a brave thing to do, Karl thought. Though this ship was only about half as tall as the *Titanic*, if that, the climb up the rope ladder still looked daunting.

"Be careful, Sallie," said Mr. Beckwith.

The crewman put a rope around her waist to secure her and she removed her high-heeled shoes, which she feared would be slippery. She must have been as scared as the rest of them, but she climbed right up the ladder, making it look as easy as could be. Once at the top she yelled back down, "It's very easy girls, you can do it!" Karl was impressed. He had never seen this side of her before.

The rest of the women followed. Helen, still unable to say a word, followed immediately after her mother. Mrs. Kimball slipped once but composed herself quickly and found the rope again. One by one they disappeared out of the boat.

Karl was the last of his group. The climb was easy for him – his athletic limbs were still moving well. When he reached the top of the ladder, a crew member helped hoist him over the side of the ship and Helen fell into his arms. He hugged the rest of his group, even Mrs. Beckwith.

"Welcome to RMS *Carpathia*," a stewardess said.

Slowly he turned around to see what was left of the scene they had lived through. He scanned the Atlantic Ocean, where their ship had been effortlessly floating the night before. Lifeboats were all that was left. Lifeboats and icebergs. His heart sank when he realized there was more of the latter than the former.

He knew how lucky they were to be on board this ship, to be safe and healthy – to be *alive* – but as Helen sobbed into his shoulder, and he clung to her tightly, he couldn't help but think that this wasn't what lucky was supposed to feel like.

Far off on the horizon Dick could see a boat. His fellow passengers who also clung onto the half-submerged lifeboat through the night began to perk up as they saw this ship stop and begin to load people from other lifeboats onto their deck. They were being rescued. They were going to survive. Dick felt his eyes watering up and finally allowed himself to look around his boat and meet the others eye to eye, to know that he was not alone. He wasn't sure if his tears were of loss or hope, despair or happiness, but it didn't really matter anymore. The tears were no longer something to hide. They were another sign he was alive.

The sun was coming up. It was a new day. With the sunlight guiding their way, the closest lifeboat came to pick up those in Dick's collapsible. Lifeboat 14 had not been so far off. It seemed so cruel that it hadn't come earlier last night, back when they were counting to ten just to stay alive, back when the man hanging onto Dick's shoulder was still alive. Back when there were twenty of them. Now there were fourteen.

It was surprisingly difficult to climb into the lifeboat. For the first time he noticed just how cold his legs and arms were. It felt like his bones had turned into ice. He had to get help to stand up and was practically dragged on board the lifeboat. He was concerned when his legs and arms felt just as cold out of the water as they had been in it, but for the time being he decided not to dwell on it. He was alive. The pain was a reminder of that. He should be thankful.

He scanned the faces of the people on the lifeboat, hoping he would see some of his friends or anyone he recognized. And while he didn't see any of his friends from the ship, he found a lot of familiar faces – familiar, but horribly altered. They all sat in silence, looking to their laps, their fine clothes and hair worried, their faces swollen, pale and wrinkled. These were not the same people who had boarded the White Star liner four days ago.

Dick debated over and over in his mind whether or not the ship that seemed to be coming towards them at a snail's pace was just a mirage. Every time he thought it was getting closer, the ship would stall for what seemed an eternity. While the bit of logic that was left in his brain assured him that the ship was stopping to pick people up, another part of his mind was convinced he was imagining the whole scene.

In fact, the reality of the situation was a long way away from sinking in for Dick. But as he sat in an upright position in a lifeboat for the first time and saw a ship coming towards him, presumably to rescue him from this nightmare, it became more and more apparent that there wasn't going to be any waking up from this nightmare. This was a different wait, a different hope than he had ever experienced before. This was about survival, about food and shelter, about having the chance to live another moment.

The pain was beginning to overwhelm him. As he sat there trying to imagine the good things that were going to come on the ship – warm clothes, food, a place to sleep – he began having a harder and harder time blocking out the intensity of the pain and the memories from the previous night. He pictured his father on the exercise bike. He thought about standing on the bridge with the captain. He hadn't imagined then that he would ever feel anything like the pain he had in his arms and legs now.

His mind went to the smokestack, the one that killed his father and blew smoke right in his face. The smokestack that he had so marveled at when he first laid eyes on the ship, the smokestack that had seemed to rise right into the sky. He hoped that his father didn't feel any pain and that he didn't realize what was happening to him, He hoped that he was at peace.

"Sir? Sir, are you okay? Can you move? Do you need help?"

Dick didn't realize that the rescuers had finally arrived. The wait was over. He opened his eyes, and though the world was blurry, he could make out the faces of crew members that he assumed were from the other ship. It took him a minute to fully process what they were asking him. A ladder was hanging down the side of the ship and he could see a member of his lifeboat making the climb up with apparent ease. The ship's engines were loud but welcoming. Faces peered over the sides of the deck looking down at him.

"Sir, we can pull you up if you don't think you can climb."

Dick knew what he had to do. There were people around him in much worse shape than he was. As cold and tired as he was, he knew he had to make his way up that ladder. Just as he held on for all the people who didn't make it, he knew he had to make this climb.

As painful as he imagined it would be, the reality of the ascent up the ladder was much worse. Every step up every rung felt like a thousand knives were stabbing him in the leg. He thought that as he moved, the pain would lessen. He thought that his legs would warm up and get used to functioning again, but the pain only became worse.

Passengers watching over the side shouted encouraging words, cheering each step he took. These were greater cheers than he had ever received on a tennis court. It was the first time he truly felt like he deserved applause. He knew that rung by rung, one by one, he would be able to make it up that ladder, over to the other side, to a future, no matter what that meant. He finally reached the top of the ladder and was hoisted over the side of the ship. While a massive sense of relief enveloped him, the pain in his legs was still excruciating.

A crew member of the *Carpathia* took Dick under his arm and half-carried, half-dragged him into a lounge radiating a warmth more divine than he ever before felt. The man situated Dick at a table and without a word he poured him a glass of brandy. Dick thought back to his futile quest for brandy the night before with his father and remembered the ridiculous bartender who had refused them the drink because it broke the rules. Where was all that precious liquor now? At the bottom of the sea. He felt for the flask his father had given him but realized he had lost it when he had taken off the fur coat in the water. He had to choke back tears.

The first sip of brandy was magical. He could feel it fill every crevice in his body, bringing it back to life and numbing the pain at the same time. The fatigue was temporarily lifted, the cold drifted away and the pain in his legs lessened.

"Are you going to be okay, sir?" the kind man asked, and for the first time in many hours Dick actually felt like he was going to be.

The man pointed out the dining saloon and Dick insisted on walking himself there. His walk was closer to a hobble. The dining saloon was filled with *Titanic* survivors, though at first glance Dick didn't see anyone he knew. He was served a breakfast of hot eggs, hotcakes, bacon and bread. He couldn't remember food ever tasting as good.

Numbed by the brandy and warmed by the food, he was suddenly overcome with the desire to sleep. There was hysteria all around him as grief-stricken, exhausted and injured people began to process what had happened to them. Dick knew he could not handle it yet. He couldn't think clearly. He wasn't ready for this new world. He just needed to sleep. He didn't want to bother anyone. He could already tell that the crew on board the ship, while extraordinarily accommodating, were overwhelmed themselves and had no time for him. He saw a space between a stove and the wall and thought of the warmth and the coziness. He hobbled over, collapsed to the ground and fell immediately asleep.

13

Karl did not need an invitation to join the Beckwiths and Kimballs at breakfast on this morning, April 15, 1912. After arriving on the ship, they had all been taken to the dining room where the *Carpathia* kitchen staff cooked them the most delicious breakfast any of them had ever tasted. They sat there in silence, eating, enjoying and thanking God that they were there at all. Helen was not with them. She had been unable to calm down since getting on board the ship, so Karl got her settled into a room that one of the ship's passengers generously offered. He could tell that Mrs. Beckwith was relieved that her daughter was safe and taken care of.

He could overhear women and men bawling, people hysterically searching for loved ones, looking over the edge of the ship hoping they would see their husband or father come up on the next lifeboat, and at the same time terrified they would see something they didn't want to see floating in the water – a familiar bracelet or hairpin or collar that would reveal the unthinkable.

Mrs. Beckwith was a beacon of strength and Karl couldn't help but admire her. She had been consoling Mrs. Warren for the better part of two hours and was helping get her enough brandy to numb her sorrow as she began her grieving for her husband. As for Mr. Beckwith and the Kimballs, they were in a complete daze, along with most of the people in the dining hall. There seemed to be two states of survivors, numb or hysterical. Karl wondered if any of them would ever be able to adjust and live at peace. He wondered if this dichotomy would come to define the rest of their lives – an endless alternation between feeling nothing and feeling everything.

Increasingly restless, he walked back out onto the deck, with a full stomach and a head that needed to be distracted. They had been on the ship for about four hours and there was only one lifeboat left to rescue. The *Carpathia* maneuvered the cold waters of the Atlantic with great skill, slowly and carefully rescuing those still in lifeboats, and above all craftily dodging icebergs so that there was not another accident. It was hard to believe that there were still people out there, still freezing, still suffering. It was even harder to believe how few people were out there.

How was it possible that the *Titanic* had so few lifeboats? How would his life have been different if he had known this? Would he have climbed in with Helen anyway, insistent on being with her, or would he have sacrificed himself for the sake of others? The thought that he took a spot in a lifeboat that could have been filled by a woman or child was unbearable. But no, there was no one left at that moment, and the lifeboat would have been lowered half empty anyway. He wanted to think that had he known all the facts, had he realized the severity of things, that he would have been a hero, but was that really the case?

Such thoughts were futile, but he couldn't get them out his mind. There he was, healthy, having survived this disaster with everything he wanted – Helen's love and even, apparently now, the support of her parents, but what happened now? Happiness now felt like an impossible epilogue.

When he reflected back on the circumstances of the past few months, he had a hard time recognizing himself. He used to be a leader, a caretaker for his family and a kind and generous man. But he abandoned all in pursuit of Helen. Besides his sister Gertie, he failed to keep up with his family, a fact he was deeply ashamed of. His father's health was fading and his older brothers were starting families. He emotionally removed himself from all of that the more he obsessed over his relationship with Helen. His interest in tennis, which was always his passion, had waned as he sacrificed practice and tournaments to follow her around the world. He stopped keeping his eyes open to situations where his leadership was needed. Without even realizing it, parts of himself that he had admired for so long, things that he had considered his greatest qualities, had disappeared. Perhaps this cataclysm could be the force that would jolt him back into a position of responsibility and self-respect, even as it secured him his greatest goal.

Dick jerked awake. Where was he? The sharp pain in his legs and the heat of the stove reminded him. For a moment, upon awakening, he wished it was a nightmare. His arms felt much better, but the throbbing of his legs drowned out any coherent thoughts he had. He pulled up a leg of his stiff, salt-encrusted pants and almost passed out at what he saw – his legs were turning purple. He had to get up and start moving. He had to get blood circulating through his legs again.

He pulled himself up quickly. He had to bite his own lip to keep from screaming in pain. He took a step. It hurt more than he remembered, but he was sure that it would get better if he just kept moving. One time during a tennis match, he twisted his ankle and thought he would have to retire, but his father encouraged him to keep trying. Sure enough after a few more rallies, it loosened up. This would be the same.

He wasn't sure how long he was asleep and was eager to make it to the deck of the ship to assess the situation. It wasn't that far away. As he made his way slowly, painfully, he gained a newfound appreciation for simplicity. There was nothing fancy about the *Carpathia*. There was no Grand Staircase, no endless maze of corridors, no walls too fine to touch. He merely had to hobble down a small hallway and out a door and he was right back on the deck he had so triumphantly reached that morning. He hung on through the night. He made it up that ladder when he couldn't feel his legs. *He could do this.*

With every step, the pain only became more and more unbearable. He tried to prop himself up against the wall while he walked but it didn't help. The sounds from the deck were getting closer but ever less reachable. The pain began to take over his entire body. His vision was getting blurry. His head began to throb. This wasn't working. He wasn't going to be able to walk this off. He needed to find a doctor, but first he had to sit down for a minute and rest. He leaned against the wall and slowly lowered himself to the ground.

"Are you all right? Do you need any help?"

Dick felt a hand on his shoulder, shaking him awake, but he hadn't even realized he'd been asleep. He opened his eyes and blinked a few times, trying to jerk the world around him into focus. He was still sitting in the corridor against the wall, but there was someone else. How long had he been there?

"Hey, can you hear me?"

The voice was coming from right next to him. He turned his head and the man began to come into focus, but he didn't believe what he was seeing – right there squatting next to him, checking up on him, was Karl Behr! He needed to compose himself quickly.

"I'm fine," he said, struggling to find his voice.

"Can you stand up?" Karl asked him.

He shook his head.

"Don't worry. I'm going to find someone to help you. I'll be right back," Karl said as he ran off.

Dick must have fallen asleep again, because the next thing he knew he was being carried through a hallway of the *Carpathia* by Behr and another man. They entered a private bedroom and the two men put him down gently on the bed.

"The ship's doctors are all busy," said Karl, "but I found Dr. Martin here, who's a passenger." Karl gestured to the balding, portly, middle-aged man beside him, who smiled and nodded.

"What's your name, son?" Dr. Martin asked.

"Dick Williams."

"Well Mr. Williams, let's get rid of these trousers and see just what we're dealing with."

Oh no. He was going to have to take his pants off in front of *Karl Behr*. He was mortified, but he knew there was no other way. The pain was only getting worse. He leaned on Karl as the doctor shimmied the pants off. His legs were still a horrible hue of purple.

"I was in the water. All night," he said. It was odd to hear it out loud.

"Well, Mr. Williams, it looks as though you have a case of frostbite and I'm worried you could get hypothermia. Due to the severity of the injury, as well as the implications involved, I think our best bet is to amputate," Dr. Martin said, attempting to cover up the horrible news with excessive cheeriness. "It could just save your life."

"No!" Dick exclaimed, before he could even think. He couldn't lose his legs. The idea hadn't even occurred to him.

"I know it's a lot to take in," said the doctor, "but you shouldn't worry. They have an excellent surgeon on board who..."

Dick couldn't even let the doctor finish the thought. "Doctor, I cannot lose my legs." He looked at Karl, begging him to help out. "I ... need them." A thousand things went rushing through his mind at once. He'd have to go to Harvard in a wheelchair. His uncle's house in Pennsylvania had lots of stairs. How would he even get to his uncle's house? How would he do anything? He would be dependent on other people for the rest of his life.

Then, of course, there was *tennis*. He was now faced with the possibility that he would never be able to play the sport again. It was the only thing he wanted to do. He wanted to hit a serve and run in for a wild volley winner. He wanted to play a five-set match in front of thousands of spectators, to run himself and his opponent around the court until they both dropped from exhaustion. He needed to be able to play tennis. It was who he was. He began blurting out words, hardly knowing what he was saying: "Mr. Behr, I'm a tennis player like you. I saw you on the train...didn't want to bother you...I am an admirer...I'm a player, Mr. Behr...my father...was bringing me back to America...we were going to play all the big tournaments, even the Nationals at Newport. He died on the ship...I have to play tennis....I *have* to play tennis!"

Karl stared at Dick all through his delirious outburst.

Then he turned to the doctor. "Doctor, with all due respect, surely there's another way."

"Well, if he refuses the amputation then the only thing he can do it try to keep walking, to circulate the blood. I can't guarantee that will work, though," Dr. Martin said.

"Walk? That's all I have to do?" Dick cried out.

It didn't sound like much of a choice: amputation or walk. He didn't take in the part about no guarantee of it working. Then he remembered the pain from earlier, how he couldn't even make it from the kitchen to the deck.

"You would need to walk constantly," said the doctor. "Every two hours for at least thirty minutes at a time, even through the night. You're going to need someone to help you, especially today. Are you traveling with anyone?"

He dropped his head. "I *was*," he said. He was all alone.

"I can help," Karl chipped in, smiling sympathetically.

"You don't have to," said Dick, remembering how much it hurt, realizing how hard this was going to be.

"I want to. Let me help you, Dick Williams. Let's save your legs."

That was all Dick needed to hear. He didn't know why Karl was being so nice, or why of all people on the ship he was the one to help him, or whether or not he was really going to be able to walk his legs back to life. But he knew he was going to try. He had not held onto a collapsed boat for six hours just to give up now. It was going to be awful, but it wouldn't be as awful as a life without his legs. Without tennis. Without freedom.

Karl held out his hand and Dick grabbed it. He took a deep breath and let the pain of standing up wash over him. He clenched his jaw, closed his eyes and steadied himself against

Karl's frame. He could do this. He reached down and pulled up his pants, which were now so stiff from the salt water that they barely stayed around his waist. He looked at Karl and nodded.

Together, slowly, they took a step. And another one. And another one. Two minutes later they were out of the doctor's room.

"What do you do when you're down two sets to love, Dick?"

"You get tough and never give up?"

"That's right! You take it one point at a time. One step at a time. Let's go."

14

Karl stifled a yawn. He refused to let Dick see how tired he was. He had barely slept in two nights and had not sat down since he climbed on board the *Carpathia* five hours ago. He had been practically carrying a grown man, taller than himself, for the past thirty minutes. Every part of his body was beginning to ache. But the pain that the man next to him was enduring was so much greater than his own that he felt guilty for feeling it at all. He would not stop. And it was almost a relief to be dealing with a problem outside of his own troubles – and so much greater.

He and Dick slowly made their way out to the deck of the ship. The scene there was harrowing. Babies cried. Women were hysterical. Men stood by stoically. A group of women crowded over the edge of the ship shouting the names of their husbands and children at the lifeboat below. It was the last one left in the water. This was their final hope. Some of them refused to stop believing even after the lifeboat was empty. They ran through the decks, shouting their loved one's name, pleading for any information. Nobody wanted to tell them the only thing left to tell: they were widows.

An Italian woman, who must have been from steerage class judging from her dress, came running by clutching her crying baby in her arms, screaming out for her husband and her other child. Though few understood Italian well enough to make out her words through her sobs, many ran to her to try in vain to comfort her.

Even the moments of joy were hard to watch. One woman, so overcome with happiness at being reunited with her children, lay down on top of them on the floor, as if to protect them. They cried and she had to be pulled off of them before she hurt them.

Meanwhile, Karl tried to keep his focus on Dick. He had to keep his frame firm and concentrate on small steps. He couldn't imagine the pain the boy must have been feeling. He could feel him fighting back screams every time they made a step. He kept yelling out encouragement, wishing he could do more. To lose your father and have to fight for your legs on the same day made Karl's own problems seem trivial.

But at that moment, holding onto Dick and helping a stricken man to walk to save his legs, he felt better about himself. He was making a difference and doing something more important than pining for his elusive love. As their pace picked up ever so slightly and he felt Dick put more and more weight on his own legs, he knew that this was going to be a comeback victory for the young Williams.

After the last lifeboat was rescued, the *Carpathia* remained in the area for a while, carefully and methodically gliding through the field of icebergs to make sure that they weren't missing any survivors. Passengers from both ships crowded *Carpathia's* decks looking at the icebergs and scanning the seas for any more signs of life. Rumors ran rampant – there was one iceberg that was shaped like a "V" and Karl overheard a boy saying that the *Titanic* had gone straight through it. Another woman pointed out an iceberg that looked like a giant shelf and said that it had torn off the entire bottom of the ship. Karl didn't want to know what iceberg it was or think about how the ship had gone down.

It couldn't change anything. He just wanted to get out of there.

The *Carpathia* passengers went out of their way to be helpful. Karl was able to get clean and dry clothes for both of them to wear. Someone gave Dick a pair of shoes to help him walk since he had come on board barefoot. The two went to the barber shop on deck and got their hair cut and they were able to find a hot bath for Dick to soak his legs. They did most of this in silence – Dick seemed to be in too much pain to carry on a conversation and Karl couldn't think of a damn thing to say. What good was small talk in a moment like this?

There was a moment of panic when the engines shut down – survivors eyed each other, feeling a communal flashback to the moment, less than twelve hours earlier when the *Titanic* went silent. But a steward announced that it was just for a memorial service in the first-class lounge. There were actually consecutive services – first a sea burial for the three dead bodies they had brought on board and then the memorial for the family, friends and colleagues who had died in those waters overnight. By that time the crew had done the accounting: over fifteen hundred had died. There was no more hope for the hysterical women who had been screaming their husbands' names over the side of the ship. They had said goodbye on the *Titanic*, just as he had almost done with Helen. They had said goodbye without knowing it was the final one.

Dick didn't want to go to the memorial service, so they stayed on the deck, continuing their journey step by step, grimace by grimace. Finally the *Carpathia's* engines started back up and the ship charted a course eastward, toward New York. For one last time Karl looked out at that nondescript piece of ocean where the *Titanic* and over a thousand of her passengers had vanished. Leaving them behind felt cruel, but there was nothing else to do. They had to move on – step by painful step.

A hot bath, clean clothes, a haircut, and three excruciating hours of walking on his frostbitten legs did wonders for Dick. He was beginning to walk a little faster. The events of the last twelve hours were, however, beginning to catch up with him. He was hoping to get some time alone as he didn't want to get emotional in front of Karl, who had already done so much for him. However, Karl insisted that he join him and his family for lunch. There was no hope of solitude here anyway. *Carpathia* was a fourth of the size of *Titanic* and the 705 survivors nearly doubled its population.

Karl's family – or rather, his girlfriend Helen's family – seemed like remarkable people to Dick. Mr. and Mrs. Beckwith spent the entire morning in the first-class lounge and on the decks comforting women who lost their husbands. He figured it must take a special person to deal with others' grief like that. Just sitting inside the dining saloon, surrounded by hysterical women, unnerved him.

"So, Mr. Williams, where are you from?" Mrs. Beckwith asked.

"I'm from Geneva, but I'm an American. I'm headed to Philadelphia and then Harvard in the fall. And please," he added, "You can call me Dick."

"I lived in Geneva for a few years when I was young," Karl said.

"Really? I didn't know that about you, Karl." It was truly surprising. His father seemed to know every connection between Geneva and tennis, but he somehow missed this one.

"We didn't know that about you either Karl," Mrs. Beckwith said, somewhat harshly, it seemed to Dick. "I presume from that statement that you are a tennis fan, Dick?" Her tone did not convey a fondness for the game.

But Dick couldn't have cared less. The only opinion at the table which mattered to him was Karl Behr's. "I am, Mrs. Beckwith. In fact, I'm a big admirer of Mr. Behr here. I have been following his tennis career for years."

Karl then turned to the rest of the table and said, "Dick here is modest, but he's an up-and-coming player himself. Once we get his legs in shape, I expect to see him on the tournament circuit this summer."

The pain in Dick's legs dampened his pleasure at Karl's statement. "If I still have my legs, that is," he tried to joke.

There was an awkward pause. "My father loved the sport," he continued. "He planned on entering me in all those tournaments this summer. Watching me play was his greatest pleasure." He couldn't stop the tears from welling up.

"Don't you worry, Dick," said Karl. "You'll play tennis again soon." He sounded more confident than Dick thought he should have been. Dick was no fool. He knew his odds at that point were not too good.

"I do believe you'll make it," Mr. Beckwith chipped in. "And remember, you'll always have your father supporting you, helping you achieve your goal, even if he's no longer there in person."

—◦◦◦—

Karl collected a tray of food to bring to Helen for dinner. She had been asleep since they got on the ship and Karl was getting more and more worried about her. It wasn't like her to get so emotional or to hide away. Before this trip, he had never even seen her cry. Of course, this was utterly new experiential territory. He was, in a way, glad that she'd been secluded that morning so she didn't have to see what was going on. He was grateful she'd be spared some of these memories.

He was also glad that he had a little bit of time away from her since he was struggling so much with his own feelings. Being a surviving man on the *Carpathia* gave him no honor.

After lightly knocking on her door he realized that the room was open and snuck in quietly, trying to not wake her or startle her. But when he looked up he saw that she was wide awake, sitting in the middle of the bed, sobbing uncontrollably.

Karl put the tray of food down on the floor and climbed into bed next to her, wrapping his arms around her tightly. "Oh Karl," she cried. "I feel so foolish. I just can't stop!" He took her head in his hands and grabbed a handkerchief and wiped her tears, pulling her hair out from in front of her face so that she could look him in the eyes.

"You, my love, have nothing to feel foolish about." He kissed her on the forehead gently and her tears subsided for a moment. He fluffed the pillows and lay back onto the bed, with her wrapped in his arms. It was the first time he had laid down at all since the previous night. He felt as if his body would melt into the bed.

"I just can't believe that it happened. All those women out there without their husbands. They're all being so strong. I don't know what I would have done if you hadn't gotten into that lifeboat. And yet, here we are, perfectly healthy and I still can't stop crying."

Karl continued to stroke her arm. She nuzzled closer to him, not wanting to be able to lose this feeling. He thought of the events of a couple of nights ago, when he had refused her advances, and wondered if he would have done the same thing if he had known that might be their last chance. It so nearly *had* been their last chance. But here they were, in bed together again, with tears and embarrassment and fatigue of an entirely different kind.

He knew that he should serve her the food that was sitting on the floor a few feet away and that he should talk to her about his feelings. He felt he had to go back and check on the others. But, at this moment, it seemed the only thing his body would let him do was sleep.

Step. Step. Step.

It was late afternoon and he was on his own. Dick knew he had to figure out how to walk without help, especially since he was under such strict instructions to keep walking no matter the pain or fatigue. It was already much easier than it had been a few hours ago, when he was barely able to put any weight on his legs at all. When he took a hot bath earlier in the day, he noticed that the coloration on his legs was improving slightly, a sure sign that progress was being made.

In a strange way he felt like this assignment was a blessing.

The focus on walking and keeping his legs alive was preventing his mind from getting distracted by the reality of the situation. There was no time for sadness or depression, regret or grieving. He had a tangible goal, a solid task to occupy his days and his mind.

The pain was still substantial. Even now, despite the marked improvement, every step still produced torturous pain. It took every ounce of strength in him not to go curl up behind the stove again, a flask of brandy in hand, and sleep through the next few days. But, if he had learned anything in the past day – the longest day in a lifetime – it was that he had a stronger desire to survive than he ever would have guessed. Perhaps he had *passion* after all. He just had to keep holding on to the railing, stay on his feet, and move his legs forward one step at a time.

Step. Step. Step.

"Dick! Dick!"

A familiar voice called his name and, before he knew it, Jack Thayer was wrapping his arms around him. He couldn't believe it. He was overcome with happiness – followed quickly by pain.

"Ow, be careful." Dick said, motioning to his legs.

"Oh, I'm sorry Dick, are you okay?"

"I'm fine, I'm fine, just need to walk out my legs is all."

He couldn't wipe the smile off his face. It was so good to see his friend. He assumed Jack met the same fate as the rest of their group. But there he was. *Alive.*

Jack just kept looking up at him, grinning from ear to ear. Dick was suddenly struck by how young Jack looked. As awful as this disaster was for Dick, he couldn't imagine dealing with such tragedy at Jack's age. After all, Jack lost his father too. For the first time, the four years between them felt significant. He felt a desire to shelter his friend from the horror, but he knew he could not.

He thought about Mr. Thayer, always the life of the party. Though Dick had struggled with him a bit this trip because of the squash match, he always admired the man and he knew how close he and Jack were. He didn't know what to say to his friend – there was so much to talk about, so much he feared talking about – that he just stood there smiling at him.

"Did you get in a lifeboat?" Jack asked eagerly, clearly wanting to break the ice.

Dick shook his head.

"Me neither," said Jack, his demeanor tightening a bit. "What about your dad?"

Dick shook his head again.

"Same here. At least, I don't think he did." There was a hint of hope at the end of Jack's sentence. Dick hated that he had to be the one to dispel it.

"He didn't Jack. I saw it."

Jack turned around to hide his face.

"I'm so sorry." Dick reached his free hand out and patted his friend on the back.

"My mom made it, but she won't talk," Jack said. "She's upset about my dad since he is not on the ship. Was it bad?"

"He was very brave," Dick said.

"What about Harry and the rest of the guys?"

"I think it's just us, Jack. Just you and me."

Jack looked away, clearly trying to hide the fact that he was wiping tears away, trying to keep his composure in front of his friend. The lump in Dick's throat was growing, but he was determined to keep control of his emotions. He had not broken down yet and he knew he needed to be strong for his friend.

Dick reached out and put his arm around Jack and leaned on him. It reminded him of the way he reached for his father a few nights earlier, looking out that porthole and thinking everything was perfect. Already Dick knew that everything about that life was gone.

"You need some help walking?" Jack asked, his voice only slightly wavering. As much as Dick wanted to be alone right then he realized that Jack needed him as much as he needed help walking.

"That would be nice, Jack."

Jack positioned himself beside him, grabbing on tight to his friend, and they walked the length of the ship in silence. That was always the nice thing about Jack. He didn't have to say anything. They could just be comfortable together. They walked right through dinnertime and into the evening.

Step. Step. Step.

"I guess we're pretty lucky, huh Dick?"

"I guess so, Jack." Lucky sure didn't feel the same as it had a day ago, but he knew his friend was right.

15

Finally, after dinner, it was time for the longest day to end. For most *Titanic* passengers this was their first chance to sleep in a bed in two days. The passengers and crew of *Carpathia* were doing all they could to accommodate and comfort the survivors. Many of them gave up their beds or let people use their spare beds. Most of the private rooms went to women with children, while the women without children were put in the dining saloon. Men were quartered in the smoking room. There weren't enough mattresses for everyone so some rolled up blankets or towels or rugs. Sofa cushions from the lounge became pillows. When space in their designated rooms was scarce, people just slept anywhere. One elderly woman slept on a bench on the deck with her sister curled up on the floor right beside her. Some found beds in the crew's quarters while others curled up on towels in the bathroom. Most had been offered a change of clothes by *Carpathia* passengers, but some still went to sleep that night clothes stiff from ocean salt. They were just grateful to be alive and to have a chance to sleep, if their grief would allow it. Sleep, for many of them, offered the only solace.

The arrangements were ideal for Dick. There was no fear of getting too comfortable and sleeping through the night, thus putting him in danger of forgetting to keep exercising his legs. The smoking room was located on the main deck so he could easily walk a familiar path throughout the night without having to struggle with stairs.

Every two hours, he was up walking.

He wasn't sure whether the pain was subsiding or whether he was just getting used to it. As the hours passed, his thoughts began to clear. He stopped trying to distract himself from reality and began to process what happened over the last twenty-four hours. How was he supposed to get over a day when hundreds of people, including his father and friends, died and yet he was able to survive against all odds? Jack called them lucky and that seemed to make sense at the time, but was there somehow more to all of this? Was there any rhyme or reason to who lived and who died, or was it all as random and as heartless as it seemed?

His father, though not reserved about many things, was always a quietly religious man. He didn't go around preaching to others and never liked to initiate a conversation about it himself, but when Dick was a child they had said prayers as a family on a nightly basis. Dick often found his father saying a prayer to himself before one of Dick's tennis matches or before he tried a big case in court. God was a part of his life.

It was hard to believe in God in a time like this, to think that someone was up there just watching this all happen – or even worse, orchestrating it – but at the same time the fact that he had survived the night, and was seemingly on his way to having healthy legs again, was nothing short of a miracle. How could he believe the second part without accepting the first? How was he supposed to go on?

His father was dead. He would never see him again.

It didn't seem real.

Harry and George Widener, John Thayer, Major Butt, Francis Millet, William Dulles, Thomas McCawley and Captain Smith – they also were dead. He was with them all the previous night and now, like so many others, they were gone.

He didn't know quite how he should be reacting. He was surrounded by grieving and hysterical people, but that response wasn't natural to him. Tears weren't coming. Charles wouldn't have wanted him to grieve, that was for sure. He would just want him to keep fighting. All he had wanted in life was for his son to have the opportunities to do the things that he couldn't. That was it.

He thought back to how excited his father would get when talking about tennis. His voice would become high-pitched and pulsate with energy. He'd start fidgeting, using his hands in great gestures, imitating strokes and gaits of top players, motioning through entire games and sometimes, when he had a whisky or two in him, entire matches. It was amazing to watch a grown man turn into a little boy because he was just so passionate about something. And that's the passion that Harry had been talking about.

16

As the sun rose on the *Carpathia* on the morning of April 16, so did the realization that nothing had changed. For the survivors of the *Titanic*, their former lives, comforts and securities were gone forever. The loved ones that were lost were not coming back. The memories were not going away. There was no going backwards. Time was moving on and days would continue to pass.

Everyone dealt with it in different ways. Helen finally got herself together the evening before and gave her bed up to a grieving woman. She and her mother spent the morning consoling the widows and helping care for the children. Some of the women wanted to talk about what had happened. Others did not. There was no right or wrong way to deal with it. They just held their hands and listened.

Some men tried to put together all of the facts from the disaster, hounding Officer Pitman and other White Star employees who survived for any details they could remember. Some were certain that people were shot while going to the lifeboats. Others claimed that Captain Smith was drunk at the dinner thrown by the Wideners the night before and that was why the ship sank. Many were certain that there were iceberg warnings. Officer Pitman confirmed the truth of that last rumor, which naturally angered a lot of the people. It could have been prevented. All of this could have been prevented.

Some passengers made up stories, trying to outdo one another as to who suffered the most. Being together now was difficult for everyone. The *Carpathia* was so small that there was nowhere to escape. As time wore on, it became easy to lose perspective and tempers.

When one woman complained about the blisters on her hands because there were no men on her lifeboat, Dick finally lost his composure. "I was in the ice water for six hours!" he shouted. "Fifteen hundred died!" In the sad silence that ensued, he went back to his slow walking.

Quite a stir was made when a couple of *Carpathia* passengers ran through the boat waving life vests in the air – it turned out they were looking for autographs, as they had realized how big of a story this was going to be. Needless to say, that did not go over very well.

Karl wanted to do something to help. They all had two nights and three days more on board this ship together. A natural leader and organizer, he formed a survivor's committee with some of the other well-connected *Titanic* passengers – Frederic Seward, Molly Brown, Mauritz Bjornstrom-Steffansson, Frederic Oakley Spedden, Dr. Henry Frauenthal and George Harder.

Since he was fluent in three languages and had a lot of experience with fundraising, he decided to focus on helping out the steerage passengers, many of whom didn't speak English and were very confused about what was going on. He found that many of them had spent the night without blankets of any kind, so he and other committee members went from cabin to cabin asking for anything people could spare that would pass as a blanket. Since many of the children were left without clothes, Helen and a few other women spent their day sewing together blankets and towels as makeshift clothes to keep the children warm.

In talking with the steerage passengers, Karl realized how much more many of them had lost. Most were traveling with all the clothes and money they owned. They had nothing left. He overheard a woman from first class cry over her lost jewels or missing nightgown, but these people were truly desperate. They would be entering a new country in a couple of days, and, beyond the grief they were feeling for lost loved ones, they were scared of the future.

Karl and the other members of the Survivor's Committee started a general fund and went around to all of the survivors and *Carpathia* passengers collecting donations for the neediest among them. He talked with Captain Rostron, who had a message sent to White Star Line about starting a relief fund at their office and encouraged the company to make arrangements for those who were on their way. He ended up becoming something of a right-hand man for the captain, who was overwhelmed with responsibility and requests. He helped collect names of survivors and lost relatives to be radioed ahead.

And then, when he could, he checked in with Dick. He started looking forward to spending time with him, offering him encouragement and talking about the sport that they both shared. That was his escape. He was encouraged by Dick's positive attitude, by how he kept a smile on his face and how he persevered through the pain. And the more they talked, the more he found they had in common. They could talk for hours about tennis, Geneva and school. He gave Dick plenty of advice about what to expect in the U.S. tournaments and they were able to gossip about many of the players. It was impressive how much Dick knew about the game and about players he hadn't even seen yet. Dick's legs were still in bad shape, but they were slowly improving. Karl hoped with all of his being that his new friend would in fact get to play again someday. He deserved that.

But then Karl didn't know what to expect even for himself in the coming days and months. Then again, none of them did. If the last two days taught them anything it was that nothing in life was guaranteed.

That night, the *Carpathia* sailed through a powerful thunderstorm, but Dick was still out walking – and walking and walking and walking. As he paced back and forth on this deck that he had come to know so intimately, he couldn't help but let his mind drift to what lay ahead of him. He had practically been adopted as a member of Karl's group the past few days and, as lovely as it had been and as grateful as he was, he wondered if he was at all prepared for what it was going to be like after they docked. Karl and the Beckwiths would all go off and Jack would leave with his mother and be reunited with his other siblings. But Dick would be all alone. Sure, he would go stay with Uncle Norris, but they didn't have a close relationship and he could only imagine how awkward his uncle would feel having his dead brother's son staying in his house. It was just hard to imagine that being a place that ever felt like home. Would his mother move over here from Switzerland or would she insist that he move back? As unsure as he was about the future, he was certain that at this point there was no going back. He was determined to go to Harvard in the fall, assuming the finances could still be taken care of, but that made his stomach flip butterflies as well.

A loud clap of thunder startled him back to reality and across the deck of the ship he saw a man run out of the smoking room in his night robe into the rain. Dick hurried towards the figure as quickly as he could hobble. As the man spotted him, he turned towards him. It was Karl.

"Dick! I'm so glad I found you! Is Helen okay? I have to find Helen."

His friend was shaking hysterically and had broken out in a cold sweat. He was clearly having a panic attack.

"Karl, everything is okay," said Dick. "It's just a thunderstorm. The ship is okay. We're all safe." He put his arms around Karl and tried to steady him.

Slowly Karl pulled himself away and steadied himself against the railing. His face was ashen white. Between all the committee work he was doing on the ship, helping Helen and other survivors, Karl was barely getting any sleep. It had clearly gotten to him.

"Just a thunderstorm. Right." Karl slowly sat down on the bench behind him and buried his head in his hands. Dick sat down beside him and pulled out the flask of brandy he had been carrying around to help him with leg pain and cold night walks.

"I bet this will help," Dick said. Karl took a big swig. He leaned back on the bench and let out a big sigh, looking up to the sky as the rain poured down on him and the lightning flashed. He shook his hair out in the rain.

"Jesus, Dick, how are we going to deal with all of this?" Karl asked.

"I have absolutely no idea" Dick responded, honestly.

"I don't know either, friend, but I suppose we'll figure it out," Karl said.

"I suppose we will."

"You just make sure and get those legs in shape, because if you should happen to draw me as an opponent in Southampton or Seabright or Newport, you're going to need them."

Dick saw the gleam in Karl's eyes and grinned. "Yes, sir!"

"Believe me, I'll run you from corner to corner, baseline to net and back, just to make sure you've been taking care of yourself."

They had another good laugh. Though there were doubts and fears, scars both internal and external, they were going to make it to New York the following day and move on with their lives. Dick knew that in the days ahead he would feel alone. The grieving process had not even started. But for now, he had a new friend in Karl Behr and it seemed like everything was going to be okay.

17

Forty thousand people waited in silence at Pier 54 and the surrounding area on April 18, 1912 as the *Carpathia* pulled into port in New York. Karl knew he would never forget the sight. An endless sea of crying faces looked up at them as they pulled into dock, each ready to adjust their tears to happiness or sorrow at a moment's notice. It was a haunting sight, seeing so many people hanging on to their last ray of hope, knowing that this was the moment they would find out if their loved ones had survived or perished. There was no more waiting, no more denial. They were moments away from hysterical emotion on either end of the spectrum. The tension could be felt even before the ship docked.

Meanwhile, the survivors were experiencing their own gamut of emotions. They were all anxious to step on solid ground again, to be able to feel truly safe, to kiss the land and bid goodbye to the sea. Most were restless, fed up with four days on an overcrowded ship with extra guests, cramped accommodations and little free room to roam or have a moment alone. Excitement over docking in New York had been building for the last twenty-four hours.

Karl also had a sense of fear among his fellow travelers. None of them were walking off that ship the same person they had been. The things they had seen and experienced would change them forever, that much was clear, but it what wasn't so straightforward was how they would change. As they stepped off that ship, they were entering not only a scarier world, but a world in which they had to completely rediscover themselves and what mattered. It was a frightening proposition for all of them.

The crowd was silent as the ship finally put down its anchor and released the gangway to the dock. Scores of reporters waved notepads and signs, pushed in front of grieving family members and hustled to the front of the pack to make sure they were the first to get a quote. The more aggressive family members pushed back, determined to be the first sight their loved ones saw when disembarking the ship. Others, more fearful of bad news, stepped back and let them through as if they were afraid to look, as if they were desperate to cling onto their final moments of hope.

It was a chaotic scene and one that Captain Rostron had anticipated having dealt with so many press queries over the wires after the rescue. One night, the captain approached Karl and asked what they should do with the press when they got to the docks. Should the press be allowed to come onto the ship? Karl advised him not to allow such a thing, anticipating that everyone would be so emotional already and an influx of people on board would only make things worse. Though it was hard to fathom anything more chaotic than this, Karl was very glad he made the decision that he made, for it would have been exponentially worse if the press were climbing on as the passengers were trying to walk off.

Karl walked with Dick down the gangway, for even though his legs were much better by now, he was worried about maneuvering the ramp in a large crowd. Helen held onto her parents right behind him. When he stepped on solid ground, he could hear his name being called. Before he knew it, his sister Gertie pushed herself through the crowd and leaped into his arms. Tears streaming down her face, she kissed his cheek over and over again before finally turning to Helen and doing the same. He figured Gertie would be there but was shocked to see his older sister Margaret, who hadn't been very close with any of the family lately, standing right behind her also crying. Seeing his sisters again, he instantly felt more at ease, more complete. It was as if he were being reconnected with a part of himself that he'd forgotten he'd lost.

"Come on Karl, there's someone else who wants to see you!"

Gertie took his hand and dragged him away through the crowd, before he had a chance to say a proper farewell to anyone. He looked back at Dick, hating to leave him standing there alone. He motioned for Dick to come with him, but he declined and simply mouthed a "Thank You." Karl nodded, hoping his gesture conveyed his own gratitude back.

It wasn't until Karl saw the person his sister was bringing him to that the enormity of the moment finally hit him. Sitting off to the side, away from the rambunctious crowd, was his brother Frederich and his father, who was sitting in a wheelchair. His father looked so frail and small, as if he had aged a lifetime in the last few months. He was wrapped in a blanket that seemed to swallow his once towering frame. His face was pale and splotchy. Karl gave his brother Frederich a big hug, but when he went to hug his father, he realized that he could no longer stand up. The wheelchair had used to be merely a prop, a way to rest when he got tired, but now it seemed it had become a necessity. Karl looked at Frederich and Gertie, whose eyes seemed to confirm his worst fears. As he bent over to hug his father, he found himself sobbing uncontrollably.

"Welcome home, son," his father whispered. Karl was certain that he'd never leave his family again.

He knew that the news of the sinking had been all over the papers and it occurred to him that it would be tough on his family. But he had made sure his name was on the list of survivors that Captain Rostron wired through and had just assumed that that would put his family at ease. He was so focused on his duties on the ship, and with Helen, Dick and the Beckwiths, that he had not given much thought to what it must be like to be on dry land waiting for one's brother or son. Now, as he looked around at his father, brother and two sisters, he realized that they suffered with him.

18

As news of the *Titanic's* demise spread around the world, everyone was searching for answers. Rumors were rampant and plastered over every newspaper in the world, but Senator William Alden Smith from Michigan took a particular interest in the case. He sailed with and met Captain Smith a few years prior and he wanted to be sure to figure out why this had happened. On April 17 in Washington, he gathered a Senate committee and traveled up to New York to inspect the *Carpathia* and immediately begin an investigation. Knowing that Managing Director Bruce Ismay and other White Star employees were already arranging plans to get back to Britain as soon as possible, there was no time to waste.

So a mere twelve hours after *Carpathia* docked at Pier 54 in Manhattan, select Senate members, including Smith, began a seventeen-day inquiry into the cause of the *Titanic* disaster. Among the people summoned to the hearing, held in the banquet room of the Waldorf Astoria, were Ismay, Second Officer Charles Lightoller and Captain Henry Rostron from the *Carpathia*. The hearings were opened to the public and all survivors were invited and encouraged to come and give their testimonies.

Karl was among the few *Titanic* passengers who felt compelled to leave their families on their first day back on land and sit in the boardroom to hear the awful night recreated over and over again. He wanted answers too and he wanted to tell his story.

The first man to be questioned on that overcast April morning was Ismay. The managing director was in a frail state. He did not show his face on the *Carpathia*, keeping himself locked up in one of the first-class cabins. He told Senator Smith that he was only on board the *Titanic* as a passenger. It was Captain Smith's voyage. Ismay was just there to enjoy his famed ship's maiden voyage. He stated that he welcomed questioning and that the White Star Line would fully cooperate with any and all investigations. They had nothing to hide. He discussed the fact that the lifeboats on board the *Titanic* were in compliance with government requirements, verified that the ship had been fully inspected, and denied reports that the ship had been going at maximum speed, confirming that they were travelling at 75 knots when the maximum speed was 79 knots.

Ismay was asleep when the iceberg hit. He told the senators that he woke up to a slight jolt, so slight that he stayed in bed for a bit before venturing out to investigate the situation. He went to the captain's bridge, where Captain Smith informed him that the ship was badly damaged. He then went to talk with the head engineer, who confirmed this. Ismay helped lower the lifeboats and get women and children on board. He stated that he left the *Titanic* on the final lifeboat.

"Were you aware that there were women and children left on board the ship?" Senator Smith asked, his voice full of judgment. Karl began to feel nauseous in his seat as he listened.

"No, sir," Ismay answered.

"Are you aware that not all women and children survived?"

"I am now, sir. I was just a passenger on the ship, I was not working it."

Ismay confirmed that he did not see or converse with *Titanic* survivors on the *Carpathia*, stating that he gave full authority to Captain Rostron to take care of the survivors as he best saw fit. Rostron confirmed this later that day when it was his turn to be questioned by Senator Smith. The details of his story portrayed a true hero. He went full speed to the *Titanic* the very moment he got the distress call. He described how he skillfully dodged the icebergs and how he painstakingly made sure that there were no survivors left behind. He described for the committee the orders he gave his crew to make sure that all possible accommodations and amenities were provided to the survivors.

First Officer Charles Lightoller was also summoned. He told his heroic tale, which mirrored Dick's in many ways. He stayed on the ship until the very last minute, helping others into the lifeboats and doing his best to maintain order. After the ship went down, he held on to a collapsible throughout the night, waiting for help to come.

Karl was sick to his stomach as he sat in the crowded room of the Waldorf Astoria listening to the tragic stories over and over again. It seemed that the more questions that were asked, the farther they all got away from knowing the answer as to why this had all happened. They hit an iceberg. Too many boiler rooms flooded for the ship to float anymore. There were not enough lifeboats on board the ship for everyone to be saved. These were facts. These were explanations. They didn't feel like answers.

After being reunited with his family the previous night, Karl went back to his father's house in Brooklyn with them all. The house, usually in impeccable order, was a mess. It was clear that cleaning was not a priority the past few days. The kitchen and living room were flooded with more signs of his father's fading health. There were pill bottles, nurses' pamphlets and extra blankets thrown about. His father could no longer make it up the stairs to his bedroom so they had converted the office downstairs into a bedroom for him. Newspapers decrying the *Titanic* disaster were in piles all around and when he was unable to sleep that night he found himself sitting in a chair near where his father slept and reading through them all.

Many times throughout his tennis career, he had read about matches or tournaments in the paper and felt the journalist got the story wrong. He was used to the unsettling sensation of reading inaccuracies – or outright lies – in the paper about events in which he had participated. But this was an entirely new degree of unreliable journalism. Each headline contradicted another — stories ranged from everyone being saved to everyone being lost, from men throwing women off of boats to save themselves to every single man dying. There were reports about Captain Rostron ignoring President Taft's wires inquiring about Major Butt's status and rumors that the whole thing was a conspiracy.

But a particular series of headlines nearly pulled his eyes out of their sockets.

Love in the Face of Tragedy

Titanic Sweethearts: How Love Was Born Out of the Greatest Shipwreck

The papers were reporting that Karl and Helen became engaged on a lifeboat as the ship was sinking. It was being spun as a romantic fairytale, some good news for readers to cling to in the midst of so much bad. Karl was enraged.

But as he sat in the boardroom day after day, the truth about his love life seemed to matter less and less. It was clear a number of men would forever be judged by their actions during the crisis. Each day of their lives they had made thousands of decisions, but their legacy would be always tied to the few split-second decisions they made in the face of a disaster. A lifetime of achievement mattered little. Captain Rostron was a hero. Officer Lightoller was a gentleman and a brave survivor. Bruce Ismay was a coward. Those were their truths now.

Karl's stomach was in knots when it came time for Senator Smith to question him. It was suddenly the last place he wanted to be.

"Were you directed to get into the lifeboat, Mr. Behr, or were the instructions for women and children only?" Senator Smith's question hung in the air. All eyes of the room were on him. He took a deep breath.

"The instructions were for women and children only. Mr. Ismay was directing the launching. When Mrs. Beckwith came to the second lifeboat, which was hanging over the side of the ship, she turned to Mr. Ismay and asked if the men could go with her. I heard Mr. Ismay reply, "Why certainly, madam. Every one of you."

He heard himself telling the story and searched for the sense of relief he was expecting after telling the truth, but it didn't come. The man who had told him to get into the boat turned out to be only interested in saving himself. Women and children died. His truth had no currency. It did not free him from anything. No matter what other decisions he made in his lifetime, he knew that he was not a hero like Captain Rostron, nor was he a gentleman like Officer Lightoller. In his mind, that only left one truth left.

It had been almost ten years since Dick had been to Chestnut Hill, Pennsylvania to visit his uncle and namesake Richard Norris Williams. Chestnut Hill was a small, affluent town located just north of Philadelphia, named for the beautiful rolling hills it was built upon. It had originally been only farmland, but when the main line of the Pennsylvania Railroad was built, it became a popular place for prominent Philadelphia businessmen to settle and raise their families. It was quiet and while not as picturesque as Geneva, it had a similar charm about it.

Though the town was just as he remembered, his uncle's home was far more ordinary than his eleven-year-old mind had pictured it. He recalled spacious rooms and lavish decorations. Now that he'd been around the world, these rooms felt adequate and the décor more rustic luxurious. Perhaps this was just the way things were after the tragedy: nothing in the world would ever seem quite as glorious and majestic as it had before.

His uncle had a car pick him up at the train station and a hot meal prepared when he arrived. They embraced when they first saw each other, but it was a rather forced hug, one that took place only because they each felt that the other was expecting it. The fact was, he and his uncle never had a relationship as adults. He had very hazy memories of Uncle Norris, remembering him being a bit quiet, uptight and bossy – the complete opposite of Charles – but it turned out that eleven years changed that perception too. Everything about his uncle now reminded him of his father – his posture, the way the lines on his face ended in distinct points instead of fading away, the way he paced in place when he was nervous (in sweeping loops around the room), the way he perked up his chest when he was preparing to talk and hit the beginning of his sentences with zest. These similarities made it hard to be around him and he sensed his uncle felt the same way. The two men never spoke of the disaster and spent most of their time in the house in separate rooms. It was the quiet Dick hoped for, but there was nothing comforting about it.

He didn't want to sit around in silence all day. He wanted to play tennis. His hard work on the *Carpathia* had paid off. His legs were saved and he could walk normally. That, of course, was the important thing but Dick was anxious to get back on court, to see if he could do more than walk. He wanted to see if he could fulfill his father's dreams. So as soon as he was settled in (and caught up on sleep), he walked the two miles to the Philadelphia Cricket Club and started practicing.

The first time he hit a ball he was so nervous that his heart was racing. He picked an outside court, far from spectators. The pristine grass courts had just opened for the season and were a hue of perfect green. Then, as he had done thousands of times before, usually under his father's watchful eye, Dick Williams bent his knees, swung his racket around with his right hand in a perfect arc while simultaneously lifting the ball into the air with his left. He leaned forward, stretched as high as he could while keeping his left foot on the turf and struck the ball at the apex of its flight. The ball shot like an arrow to the intersection of service line and center line on the other side. It might have landed a few inches out, but that was the last thing Dick cared about. He had lost his father but he still had a gift from him: one of the best tennis serves on the planet.

Day after day he returned to the same outside court. His leg strength and movement rapidly improved and he had a better feel for the court than he'd ever had. When he was out practicing, the rest of the world faded away, his brain completely shut off. He just trusted his body and mind to work together in perfect unison. He would close his eyes and imagine the most fun and daring shot he could possibly hit and more often than not, he would find himself executing it to perfection. At last, he was completely in control.

On June 2, only *six weeks* after being told that his legs needed to be amputated, he competed in his very first tennis tournament in America: the Pennsylvania State Championships at the Philadelphia Cricket Club. He was a complete unknown to the other players in the field. In the locker room, he was surrounded by men who had many pages devoted to them in moleskin notebooks, now resting at the bottom of the Atlantic Ocean. Dick was a little bit star-struck to be in their presence. He kept to himself, quietly watching where the others put their gear in the locker room and where to go for practice and for meals. He wished that Karl were there to show him around, like they had talked about on the *Carpathia*.

To even get into the tournament, Dick had to play a preliminary round, against one W.H. Trotter, a man he knew nothing about but who looked to be pushing forty and quite comfortable with the prospect of playing an unknown kid from Switzerland in the first match. They contested their match on the sprawling lawn right in front of the clubhouse. Other matches were going on beside them and nobody was watching as Dick won 6-1, 6-1 in about thirty minutes. He also easily defeated his next three opponents: a Philadelphia millionaire named Craig Biddle, former intercollegiate doubles champ Allen Thayer, who he was happy to learn was not related to John and Jack, and the promising nineteen-year-old local boy William Tilden, Jr. Dick didn't even drop a set.

He made it to the final where he was to meet Wallace F. Johnson in a best-of–five-set match. The winner would play the 1911 Pennsylvania State champion Percy Siverd in the Challenge Round for the title. Wallace Johnson was the 1909 intercollegiate singles and doubles champion from the University of Pennsylvania and a fixture in the top ten in the *American Lawn Tennis* rankings for years. Dick knew all about him – there were numerous moleskin pages devoted to him. This would be the biggest test of his rejuvenated legs. His body was beginning to ache as the consecutive matches began to take their toll. He was concerned about his stamina.

Before the match, he found a surprise guest waiting for him outside the locker room – Jack Thayer. As he walked toward his old friend, who stood there beaming from ear to ear, he found himself tensing up. Memories came rushing over him, memories he had been suppressing. He just wanted to focus on the match.

"What are you doing here?" he blurted out, hoping he didn't sound angry.

"Dick, you're all over the local papers. I can't believe it. It's just like your dad said. You're going to be a star!" Jack said excitedly. Dick forced a smile, but he really just wanted to be alone in the locker room to prepare for his match.

"Well, thanks for coming.," he said, wishing that he meant it.

"Of course. I'm glad you're doing so well, Dick. It's amazing."

Jack's voice sounded much more mature than Dick remembered. He took a good look at Jack, suddenly realizing how much older he looked and acted. There were dark circles underneath his eyes and no sparkle behind them like there used to be. Dick felt guilty.

"Are you okay?" he asked, though he was afraid of the answer.

"Yeah, I'm okay. It's just been – well, you know..." Jack faded off.

"Yeah. I know." He hoped he sounded sincere.

But he *didn't* know. He had been so engrossed with tennis that the horror they'd been through felt like a lifetime ago. He knew that there were reasons to be sad, and he certainly hadn't forgotten the loss of his father, but he was honoring his father by devoting himself to his sport.

A large crowd gathered for the final. Word around Philadelphia quickly spread about this kid from Geneva who was running through the tournament like wildfire. And Dick was having so much fun on the tennis court that for the first time in his life he didn't mind playing in front of a crowd. In Switzerland, he always wished the people would go away and stop looking at him, but here he relished it.

He won the first two sets against Johnson with ease 6-0, 6-1, but in the third set he found fatigue catching up with him. He knew that if he lost the third set, he would be in for a fight and would be in trouble.

At 5-5 in the third set, with the crowd eager to see more tennis and urging on the well-known champion Johnson, Dick looked up and saw Jack in the crowd cheering him on. Suddenly he thought of the swim, the cold, the pain. He thought about the hours spent holding onto that lifeboat, the people who didn't make it, the hours of walking and fighting he had been through on the *Carpathia* to get him to this moment. He fought through all of that. He made it through the unimaginable. He could win this tennis match.

He anticipated Johnson's serve out wide and took the ball almost immediately after it bounced and drove it hard down the line, not giving Johnson a chance to react. This gave him a break point, and after getting a good return in play, he was able to come to net and connect with a high volley that was angled so far away from Johnson that he didn't have a chance. Dick broke serve to go up 6-5.

The crowd rose to their feet with applause, so impressed by Dick's level of play that they momentarily forgot that they had been rooting for Johnson to extend the match. They had never seen tennis played like this before – so carefree and aggressive. It seemed to come so easy to him. Dick smiled on court, soaked in the applause and let the adoration re-energize his legs. He tried to keep his mind focused. Looking across the net, he could already tell that his opponent was defeated. All he had to do was get a few solid serves in play to seal the victory. Johnson's shoulders were slumped and his eyes were darting around, clearly distracted by the crowd's excitement. Four points later, Dick hit his last un-returnable shot and walked to the net to shake Johnson's hand. After this victory, he felt like he could do anything in tennis.

The next day, Dick went on to beat defending champion Siverd 6-1, 6-1, 6-1 to win the Pennsylvania State Championships. His body was exhausted, but the match didn't last any longer than a practice set would have, so it didn't matter. Siverd had nothing to challenge Dick's game.

One tournament. One trophy. No sets lost. It was a debut unlike any tennis player had ever had on American soil.

And he was far from done. He wanted to keep playing and to keep winning. He won the U.S. national mixed doubles championship with Mary K. Browne at the Cricket Club the following week and then was invited to play the prestigious U.S. Clay Court Championships in Pittsburgh at the end of the month. With a skip in his step and some unrecognizable swagger in his stride, he sought out some clay courts nearby and began to prepare for his second singles tournament.

At the Penn States, Dick had been an invisible unknown in the locker room, but when he got to Pittsburgh, things had changed. There was a buzz everywhere he went. He could feel that other players were talking about him, inspecting him. Still, he remained calm and determined.

The human mind has an amazing ability to compartmentalize feelings and memories. In those days, Dick rarely let himself think about the *Titanic* and he never talked about it. He wanted to move on. He was building a new life for himself. But when he was on the tennis court, when he was playing those matches and steamrolling through opponents, he felt closer to his father than he ever had in his life. He didn't have to think about him or talk about him or cry for him. He was playing for him.

At the Clay Court Championships, he breezed through the first three matches with identical scores – 6-0, 6-2. By the time he reached the quarterfinals, the galleries for his matches were jam-packed, with little boys being placed on their father's shoulders to catch a glimpse of this unheralded kid. With each serve he felt more in control of his life. With each volley he felt more alive. With each win he felt more and more confident.

In the all-comers final, he met the defending national doubles champion Gustave Touchard. Dick smiled his way through the match, charming the crowd and infuriating Touchard, who was left defenseless against Dick's aggressive onslaught. He beat Touchard in straight sets and continued his winning streak in the Challenge Round, unseating the defending champion Walter T. Hayes 6-3, 6-1, 8-6.

Pennsylvania State Champion. United States Clay Court Champion. No sets lost in America. Former champions dismissed like so many schoolboy players. What had once seemed impossible now was within his grasp. Maybe, just maybe, he was as good as his father thought he was. Maybe those dreams weren't so far-fetched after all.

"He could be the next great American player," said the pundits. "He is setting a record for fastest ascent from unranked to the top ten – it only took him two tournaments!" they marveled.

"If he keeps playing like this he might never lose."

"He could beat the "California Comet" himself Maurice McLoughlin!"

"He might even win the Nationals this year."

For the first time, he actually believed that he could.

19

It was the middle of June and Karl had still not moved back into his Manhattan apartment. He had taken over the Brooklyn mansion where his father was recovering, putting himself in charge of the nurses and maids, the yard work and starting countless fix-it projects around the house. He convinced himself that he was doing this for his father and his family, as if putting in so much time at the family house would in some way make up for his self-perceived selfishness of the past few months. In many ways, it was working. His father's health was improving. The house was in impeccable condition and he felt closer to his father than he had in years. He found himself spending less time at his law firm and taking on more projects with Herman Behr & Company. His father, meanwhile, would spend the mornings lecturing him on business practices, accounting, production — anything Karl could think of to ask.

There was little time for tennis right now. Most of the tournaments required an overnight trip and he couldn't bring himself to leave his father for even a night. He practiced occasionally and planned on playing some tournaments in New York later in the summer, but for the time being he wasn't interested in putting himself into a competitive situation. Anything that took focus away from the family seemed inappropriate.

He was surprised to read about Dick's championship runs in Pennsylvania — he had no idea that he was *that* talented. There was something about it, though, that bothered him. He didn't think it was that Dick was already accomplishing things in tennis that he had never been able to – Karl had comes to terms long ago with the fact that he better as a doubles player and was satisfied with his accomplishments. It just seemed unfathomable that Dick would be able to move past the tragedy so quickly, while he himself was barely hanging on. How could Dick concentrate on the match at hand so soon after the horrific loss of his father?

Karl thought about the *Titanic* all the time. He tortured himself replaying the night in his mind, wondering if he could have done anything differently. He thought about getting into that lifeboat and couldn't help but wonder whether someone else could have been saved if he hadn't. He thought about the cries in the water – and Officer Pitman's decision not to go back. He understood why Pitman made that decision, but should he have fought it? Could he have done more?

Helen, meanwhile, was staying busy herself. She and Karl had not been seeing as much of each other. Upon returning home, she found herself quickly involved in a suffragist march going down Fifth Avenue in New York City and in fact became one of the leaders of the march. She and Karl had seen each a few times, Helen mainly talking about the marches and the movement and the politics so quickly and enthusiastically that he had a hard time getting a word in. He fell in love with her passion, so why was it disagreeable to see it in action now?

He knew what he was doing – he was distancing himself from the things he had once loved. But he didn't know how to stop or even if he wanted to. It was so odd how the things that had mattered to him the most a few months ago now seemed so trivial. The only place he felt truly comfortable was with his father in the house he grew up in – the house he barely visited in recent years.

On a hot Saturday afternoon, he was working on his latest project, putting new countertops in the kitchen. While it might have been clear to others that the project was beyond his abilities – and completely unnecessary – he was certain that he could not move out until it was done. His father just simply could not live in that house anymore until the countertops were replaced. The plan seemed to be backfiring around midday however, as the measurements were simply not lining up. He stood helpless in the middle of a kitchen full of topless cabinets, on a floor littered with loose nails and screws. His body drenched in sweat.

A knock on the door startled him, causing him to drop his hammer and send a few more nails flying around the room. The sight of Sallie Beckwith standing at the door, staring at his sweaty, disheveled form, nearly caused him to pass out. She walked in and didn't try in the least to hide her judgment and amusement over the complete disaster of a kitchen. She swatted at a fly. The friendly visage she had shown on the *Carpathia* had disappeared. He found himself staring at the same disapproving grimace that hounded him throughout Europe. He braced himself for bad news, knowing that her presence here couldn't mean anything else. Of course, he didn't have any countertops on which to brace himself.

His first thought was that something terrible must have befallen Helen, for surely that would be the only reason she would travel to his house. He was nauseated thinking about the possibility.

"Is something wrong with Helen?" he asked.

"No Karl. She's fine." Her tone was harsh and not reassuring.

He took a deep breath, relieved that Helen was okay but more confused as to the nature of this visit. He hadn't seen Sallie once since they had been back in New York, and her stopping by wasn't something he was accustomed to, especially way out in Brooklyn. But he led her through the disarray in the kitchen and into the living room, which, aside from a few stacks of newspapers that hadn't moved since April, was presentable. If only he had time to make *himself* presentable. He gestured to the sofa and offered to get her a cool beverage, but her knee was shaking a bit and it was clear that she was ready to say whatever it was that had brought her this far. He sat down on a chair opposite her, preparing himself for the worst.

"Karl, I don't want to get in the middle of things, but is everything all right between you and my daughter? She says she hasn't seen you in a while."

"Yes ma'am, I've just been busy, at work and here with my father." He hoped the table and stacks of papers were hiding the nervous tapping of his foot.

"That's what she said, but I can tell she's worried. Should she be?"

"No ma'am, there's no reason to worry."

"Listen, Karl, I know I haven't always been the nicest person to you. Helen and I are very close and the thought of her settling down so young frightened me, I must admit. But I've seen the two of you together and I saw how you acted on that ship."

She was glaring at him, pleading with him, saying the words he had longed for. He couldn't bring himself to look her in the eye. He was afraid he would lose his composure.

169

"Karl, we've all been through a traumatic experience, but we can't go through it alone."

She picked up one of the papers with a picture of Karl and Helen on it that was sitting in front of her. "Don't let this scare you away. This is just a story. It's not your story. Don't let them scare you away from your story."

Sweat poured down Dick's back as he anxiously paced around Pier 54 in New York. It was a hot day in mid July, but he never sweated this much, not even when he was playing in a tennis match. Here he was, only three months after the *Carpathia* had pulled up to this very pier, waiting for his mother's ship to come in. She instructed him to meet her at the hotel, but he thought he would surprise her. She had not been to America in fifteen years and he wanted to make sure she was safe and could get around the city. Plus, he was excited to see her.

But being back there was more difficult than he anticipated. He had done such a good job of fighting those memories, of focusing on tennis and his new life. But standing there right now, with nothing to distract him and nobody to talk to, it felt like it had all happened yesterday.

He could picture himself walking down the gangway, Karl walking with him until the bottom just to make sure his freshly working legs didn't collapse at the wrong time and leave him trampled by thousands of people. He remembered descending into that crowd, the biggest he'd seen in his entire life, and feeling like it might swallow him whole. He remembered making it to the bottom of the gangway, onto solid ground, and feeling simultaneously overcome with relief and dread. Karl's family came to greet him, dragging him away and leaving Dick alone. He was in a sea of forty thousand people and yet he had never felt so alone in his entire life. He could see the signs, hear the calls of the journalists trying to get any quotes they could. He could still hear the cries of friends and family members as they screamed their loved ones' names, hoping that if they just screamed a little louder and waited a little longer, the news they were dreading so much wouldn't come. He remembered standing in the middle of that crowd realizing that nobody was calling his name.

Though the memories were vivid, he could no longer identify with the lonely, fearful boy standing on the deck three months ago. He had rapidly transformed from the awkward and shy boy who had stepped off of the *Carpathia* into the confident man his father had always known he could be.

His back-to-back tennis titles had opened up a world of opportunity to him. He had a lot of tournaments to look forward to the rest of the summer — the Longwood Bowl, the New York State Championships, Southampton and the Nationals at Newport. Tennis experts up and down the east coast were saying that he was the only player who had a chance to threaten the top American player Maurice McLoughlin. All summer he heard his father's voice repeated in his ear: "U.S. Nationals Champion, Richard Norris Williams!" He was beginning to feel himself that this was his destiny.

But seeing the ship slowly floating up to the dock, he remembered how excited and nervous he was about seeing his mother. He hardly knew anyone in the United States. He had been on this crazy ride all by himself the past few months. What would it be like to have her here? Would it provide the comfort and familiarity that he had longed for those first few days? Did he still need that comfort?

He stood there awkwardly waiting for his mother, feeling uncomfortable in his skin for the first time in a while. He was in fear of locking eyes with her too early – how was he supposed to react? Should he run up to her and cry like so many people did? Should he wait for her to come to him? He was over-thinking every detail.

As soon as he saw her, though, all of his doubts disappeared. She looked as though she had aged about twenty years in four months. She looked so confused, so out of her element, so helpless, that he couldn't help but run to her. He was upset that she was coming to America for him, but it had never occurred to him that she might be coming for herself.

She embraced him tighter than they had ever hugged before. The hug lasted for a long time and he could feel her sob into his shoulder. He had never seen his mother cry before, nor could he really remember the last time they hugged. But as she continued to squeeze tighter and tighter he realized that it had been a long time since he had hugged anyone like this.

She looked up at him, her eyes practically the only thing about her that hadn't changed. She looked him up and down, examining his clothes – he had purchased a new wardrobe since he lost everything on *Titanic* — and his haircut, everything down to his shoes, which he just had shined.

"You've changed, my son. You have changed."

It took him a few days to get himself back together, but Karl knew that Mrs. Beckwith was right. He had let himself believe that he had to choose between Helen and his family, but he was realizing that he would not be truly happy until he had them both. His family had planned a vacation weekend at their lake house in New Hampshire, a rare time when all of his brothers and sisters and father would be in one place. This, finally, would be the perfect time to propose to her.

His mother's ring, which he had planned on giving to her, had gone down with the *Titanic*, so he was left scrambling trying to find something he could afford that she would like. Luckily, his father was excited about the proposal and willing to help out, and Gertie, after being sworn to secrecy, was able to help him pick out a perfect new ring.

Helen was taking summer classes at Briarcliff, so since he couldn't go see her in person, he sent her a telegram, reminiscent of the one she had sent him in Austria.

DEAREST HELEN STOP BEHR FAMILY
SPENDING WEEKEND AT THE LAKE
HOUSE IN SQUAM LAKE STOP PLEASE
JOIN US STOP LOVE KARL

He didn't get a response, which could have various meanings. Either she had not received the telegram, she had received it and was so upset with him for how distant he had been lately that she had declined his offer, or she was planning on coming and not telling him, just as he had done to her a few months earlier.

As Friday afternoon at Squam Lake turned into evening, he began to get more and more nervous, though he tried to hide it from his pestering siblings, who could not stop making fun of him and his attempt at romance. Frederich scolded him for not picking her up himself. Gertie was furious that he didn't call her on the telephone. Margaret was certain she was going to stand him up. Herman thought she might have come to her senses after all this time apart and Max was just enjoying watching his younger brother sweat it out. However, as they all sat on the front porch after dinner nursing cocktails and relishing the fact that the sun was setting and they were finally getting a break from the scorching heat, a car could be heard coming up their long, winding driveway.

Karl barreled down the staircase. When the car finally pulled up and he saw Helen's face in the backseat, he felt as nervous and as excited as he had the first time he saw her, staring out his kitchen window and watching her talk with Gertie. It had, in fact, been almost six weeks since they had seen each other.

She got out of the car with a big smile. She was dressed in her most casual and comfortable dress, but she looked more beautiful than ever. He was planning on kissing her and making up for lost time, but when he looked into her eyes he found himself completely frozen. He wasn't sure whether it was the embarrassment of having his siblings watching him, the shame of having been away from her for so long, or the nerves about proposing, but he was unable to move. Could he really just pick up where he had left off ten weeks ago?

Helen got along so well with his family, was so funny and charming, and loved everything outdoors. She held his father's hand when he lost his balance, went fishing with Frederich and Max, and spent hours giggling with Margaret and Gertie. The only problem was, she didn't seem to be paying much attention to him. There was a noticeable tension between them and though he was glad she was so comfortable around his family, it seemed as if maybe she was no longer comfortable around him.

He took Max aside after dinner on Saturday, knowing his loud-mouthed brother would not spare his feelings.

"Am I imagining this, Max? Is she ignoring me? What do I do?" He was out of breath and panicked.

"Karl. Get it together." His much taller sibling put his hand on his shoulder, his voice more serious and steady than he could ever recall it being before. "You need to get her alone and talk to her. It's that simple."

Karl nodded, breathing deep, knowing his brother was right. Of course Helen was ignoring him. He had been hanging back, paralyzed by fear, waiting for her to give some sort of signal while giving off no signals of his own. He had to do more than just send a telegram. He had to actually spend time with her. Why did that sound so scary to him right now? When did he become the type of person that needed to be pushed along at every corner?

He leaned against the porch railing, took deep breaths to try to get himself together. Max lit a cigarette and offered him one. While Karl rarely smoked since he began seriously playing tennis eight years ago, he took Max's cigarette and took a long, drawn out drag. He could feel Max staring at him and couldn't imagine what his brother thought of him at that moment, too nervous to even ask the girl he loved to marry him. Too nervous to even talk to her. He expected Max to begin laughing and teasing him mercilessly at any moment, but instead when he looked up at his brother he saw compassionate eyes staring down at him.

"I'm just so glad you're all right," Max said.

Karl put out his cigarette, smiled up at Max and went back inside to finally do what he came to do. He walked into the living room and saw Helen looking up at him, concerned. He figured he must have looked as desperate as he felt, but it was now or never, or at least he had to convince himself of that so he wouldn't put it off any longer. He walked over to her and quietly asked if she would like to join him on a walk. He had intended to whisper it into her ear, but his voice was a bit too shaky for whispering. She nodded cautiously.

It was a perfect, balmy summer night. There was just enough of a lingering breeze to make the humidity manageable, but the air felt still and peaceful. There was a full moon and not a cloud in the sky. Karl led Helen down the winding path that he and his brothers had helped their father build when they first purchased the lake cabin many years ago. They all still lived in the tiny Manhattan apartment at that time, but his father insisted on buying a vacation house before moving to a bigger home, saying that homes would always be chaotic no matter how big they were, but that if a family had a nice place to vacation during the summer it didn't matter. For the most part that had been the truth. The cabin had been a solace for the family throughout the years. When the children would get into big fights, his father would take a select group of them up to the cabin and put them to work building something new, convinced that manual labor and teamwork were the best medicine. When Karl's mother was sick she would spend entire weeks just sitting on the front porch starting at the water. One time towards the end of her illness, he and Gertie were able to convince her to get out onto one of their canoes. They paddled her around, watching her hand glide against the water and her face light up as the boat floated through the water. It was his favorite memory.

Karl and Helen walked side by side, but neither of them spoke for quite some time. At the end of the path was a veranda that overlooked the lake. That was where he wanted to propose. He was afraid that if he started talking now he would accidentally blurt things out before they got there. His heart was racing and his brain was spinning. He kept reaching for her hand but retracting it before she saw it, somehow afraid that feeling her touch would cause him to lose his mind altogether. He was hanging by a very thin thread.

They finally reached the veranda, still in complete silence. They sat on the bench, both looking at the water instead of each other. The view was absolutely breathtaking. The lake seemed to go on forever and the way the stars and moon reflected in the water and the gentle breeze ruffled their hair reminded him of their romantic nights on the deck of the *Titanic*. Their legs lightly touched, but it was enough contact to make his entire body shake.

He finally looked at her and she looked back at him. He realized what he was so afraid of. Helen knew him so well that when she looked him in the eyes, she could see through his brave front and see the discomfort he felt inside. He could see hers too and he realized that she was hanging on by the same thin thread he was. The guilt of being *Titanic* survivors tested their conscience. They survived a great tragedy unscathed, but to continue in life, heal and move on, they needed to do it together, not apart.

"I've missed you so much," he heard himself saying and let it sink in how true that was.

"I've missed you too." She smiled and reached for his hands.

"I'm sorry I've been so distant. I guess it's just been hard..." He was afraid to elaborate.

"For me too. But I need you Karl. I can't get through this without you." A single tear fell down her face and he wiped it away, hating himself for ever having let her being alone.

"I think about it all the time. Getting on that lifeboat, not going back to save others. Sometimes I wish I'd done things differently. "

"I know you do." She looked up at him, her eyes conveying nothing but understanding and sympathy. She wasn't judging him. She wasn't taking it personally. She wasn't trying to convince him that his feelings were wrong. She was just accepting him. She could accept him even when he couldn't accept herself. He was even more in love with her than he knew was possible.

"Your mother came to visit me the other day," he said, feeling for the ring in his pocket.

"She did? Oh no, I'm so sorry."

"No, no, it's okay. She was very helpful. It turned out to be just the thing I needed."

"I don't know if I like the sound of that," Helen laughed. It felt so good to Karl to hear her laugh.

He pulled the ring out of his pocket and showed it to her. Helen's smile rivaled the moon's illumination.

"She asked me to marry you."

Helen's smile turned to a laugh and then to tears. The good kind. The kind they hadn't cried in a long, long time.

"And, Karl, what did you say to her?"

"Well, I think I said yes, didn't I?"

She nodded, tears welling up in her eyes. He put the ring on her finger and she brought him in for a kiss that he knew he'd remember forever. They hadn't kissed that way in a long time. It was a moment of pure joy that they both wanted to hold onto for as long as they could.

"I love you so much."

"I love you too, Helen. I always will."

20

It had been a big two weeks for Karl. He was now engaged and finally moved out of the Brooklyn house and back into his one-bedroom apartment on the Upper East Side in Manhattan. Now it was time to get back to tennis. It had been ten months since he had last played a competitive match, and that loss (6-0, 10-8, 6-8, 1-6, 6-4 in the fourth round of the Nationals to Raymond Little – he'd never forget that score) haunted him for quite some time. He still finished 1911 ranked ninth in the *American Lawn Tennis* rankings though and was excited – as well as apprehensive – to see how his game had held up. Most of the other men had been playing tournaments since May, so he was well aware that he had a lot going against him.

His first tournament of the 1912 season was the Longwood Bowl at the Longwood Cricket Club in Chestnut Hill, outside Boston. He had great memories there, having made it all the way to the final back in 1906 when he was just starting out. It was nice going back and seeing his fellow players again. He was one of the elder statesmen on the circuit these days and while many of the younger men were quickly surpassing him on the court, he liked to think that they looked up to him a bit and respected his experience.

Karl had been quite taken aback by the reports of Dick's success. It was almost unimaginable to think that this kid who had been writhing around on the deck of the *Carpathia*, unable to walk, was now being hailed as the second-best American player.

He simply couldn't reconcile the player he was reading about in the papers with the young man he spent time with on board the ship, sharing his deepest secrets. He was anxious to see Dick for himself, but at the same time there was a knot in his stomach – he had imagined being the one helping Dick out, showing him the ropes and teaching him how to go about things. He should be the one inviting Dick into *his* world. But with all the hype surrounding Dick's run of success – without dropping a single set as he was always reminded — it was beginning to feel to Karl like he was merely a spectator stepping into Dick's world.

The first time he saw Dick was in the locker room at Longwood on the first day of the tournament. They both had afternoon matches scheduled that day. Karl was anticipating the meeting. The draw came out with them in the same section, meaning that if they each won two matches they would play each other.

Dick was already in the locker room when Karl walked in and the two immediately made eye contact and approached one another. Karl tried his best to be friendly and inviting, convinced that his hang-ups must have more to do with his own insecurities than anything Dick had done. But as Dick walked towards him he was hardly recognizable. He stood up straight and walked with a certain swagger of confidence. He still had that child-like grin on his face, but it exuded joy and self-assurance, not awkwardness and embarrassment like it had before.

These are all good things, Karl had to remind himself.

They shook hands, an oddly formal greeting for two men who had shared so much so recently.

"Good to see you, Dick. Congratulations on your success! I suppose we can assume your legs are feeling better!"

"Thanks, Karl. Yes, I'm fine."

"I can only imagine." That much was true. In his seven years of competitive tennis Karl had not achieved the level of success that Dick had achieved this summer.

"How's Helen doing?"

"She's fine." Karl found himself wanting to tell him about the engagement, but for some reason he stopped himself. Instead there was a long and awkward pause.

"Well, good luck out there today." Dick was smiling but looking at his locker, as ready as Karl was for the conversation to end.

"Yes. Same to you, Dick."

The two men hesitated, then shook hands again and went their separate ways. Karl couldn't believe how terribly that had gone, how hard it was to see Dick and how uncomfortable they both were. Just a few months ago, he was telling Dick his every secret. They had been so close. Was it just his jealousy over Dick's success holding him back now?

As fate would have it, Karl and Dick both advanced through the tournament to face each other in the fourth round. Karl played perhaps the most inspired tennis of his career, and dug deep to overcome a two-set deficit to upset Dick 0-6, 7-9, 6-2, 6-1, 6-4. It was the first time Dick lost a match, let alone a set, on American soil and since the *Titanic* disaster. It was Karl's biggest win in four years by far. Observers called it one of the fiercest battles seen at Longwood in many years.

After the match, Dick and Karl shook hands at the net. Dick quickly escaped the court, hastily showered, changed and left the locker room without saying a word to anyone. Karl wondered how the defeat would shape the young player in the tournaments to come and whether it would a have a lasting effect.

The consequence for Karl was an adrenaline shot of confidence. His upset over Dick led to a rejuvenated summer of results, one where he felt flashes of the game he used to possess. He lost to the eventual champion McLoughlin in the Longwood semifinals, but after an early loss in the New York State Championships, he went on to have his best showing at the Nationals in Newport in five years, making the semifinals where he lost to his old rival William Johnston. Dick's summer continued to be impressive but was marred by two extremely close losses to McLoughlin, in the final of Southampton and the quarterfinals of the Nationals.

At the end of the year, Karl found himself ranked seventh in the country, his fifth top-ten finish and the highest he'd been ranked since 1907. However, he found himself unexpectedly relieved when the tournaments were over for the year. He had a business to run and a wedding to plan.

Dick ended the year ranked second in the country, right behind McLoughlin. He was thrilled, although when he made his first steps onto the Harvard Campus that September he was still trying to recover from his loss to the "California Comet" in the Nationals two weeks before. He kept replaying the points he lost in his head, and was excited to play McLoughlin again the next season so he could implement some of the lessons he learned from his defeat. His debut summer on the tournament circuit brought many successes, more than any pundit would have predicted, more than he had ever expected.

For the first time in a long time he really felt like his life had purpose. He wanted to keep playing tennis, he loved being in front of the crowds and painting the lines with his shots. He loved travelling to new places and making new friends. He wanted to keep playing, to keep improving, and to finally win the U.S. Nationals trophy – for himself, and mostly for his father. He wondered if this inspired feeling could have been what he had been missing all along – *was this passion?*

Despite his new-found vigor he couldn't help but feel nervous as he started off on a new adventure at college. Would he like his professors? Would he be able to keep up in his classes? Would he make new friends? Luckily his mother came with him to help him get settled into his dormitory – she had moved into a house only a few miles away in the suburbs of Boston. They strolled around the hallowed campus to get acquainted and figure out where his classes were, where the dining room was, where the gymnasium was – all the essentials. His mother did her best to be helpful but they both knew was a situation that they both knew his father would be much better equipped to handle. Within minutes he would have had the entire campus figured out and he and Dick would have been sitting at dinner with the most influential people on campus.

In the heart of campus there was a giant construction site. A new building was going up and it looked like it was going to be a big one. It seemed odd for them to be starting such a big project, especially at the beginning of the school year. His curiosity led him to the plaque that had already been erected.

The Harry Elkins Widener Memorial Library.

He felt more at home already.

21

Karl's palms were sweaty, his knees were weak and his heart was racing as Richard Beckwith escorted Helen slowly down the aisle. She looked uncomfortable but stunning in her dress, a white satin charmeuse gown with an impossibly long train and elaborate lace veil. He could barely see her face, but he saw the outline of a smile, which helped him relax a little bit. Max, Frederich and Herman were all there as groomsmen and Gertie was the maid of honor. Sallie Beckwith sat in the front row crying. Karl's father just beamed. The bridesmaids wore gorgeous light pink gowns with a lace chiffon overlay, lace hats and pink bows. On this special day, March 1, 1913, the Church of Transfiguration on East 29th Street in Manhattan was decorated in Easter lilies and palms. Karl had heard more about flowers and dresses in the past few months than he ever thought possible, but he enjoyed every minute of it. It was Helen's dream wedding, and so it was his.

After so much anticipation the actual ceremony was a blur. They said vows, exchanged rings and were presented as husband and wife. For him this was all a mere formality. He had been committed to Helen since the moment he saw her. All the struggles since had only made his love for her grow stronger. He saw a glimmer of a tear in her eye as he leaned in to kiss her.

Their love would always be attached to a tragedy. Their best memories would always lead inevitably back to their worst. It was something he knew he'd struggle with for the rest of his life, but this was their reality. He began to realize that no matter what he had done differently that night on the *Titanic*, no matter how noble he had been in those moments if he had been able to foresee the future, there was no way to change their present. He did not believe that there was some divine reason why they survived and others did not. He did know that he needed to make the best out of this life and the best thing in his life was Helen.

Dick woke up in a cold sweat, panting, startled. He felt the shudder of the ship, heard the engines turn off and saw the next twelve hours of his life flash before his eyes. He had to get out of there. They had to get into a lifeboat right away. They were running out of time. The ship was sinking. He looked at the bed to his right for his father, startled when he saw someone else in his place.

It was Maurice McLoughlin.

He wasn't on the *Titanic*. He was on the *New Yorker*. Their ship was fine. Everything was okay. It was his third night on this voyage and the third night of these nightmares. He took a deep breath, closed his eyes and lay back down. Everything was all right.

It was fifteen months since that fateful night on the *Titanic* and this was his first time on a ship since the *Carpathia* docked in New York. He was on his way to Europe to represent the United States in the 1913 Davis Cup competition in Britain. Davis Cup was the most important event in tennis – the international team competition where tennis players played for their country in three-day events known as ties. Each tie was best three-of-five matches – four singles and one doubles. Just as in major tournaments of the day, the team that won the "all-comers" draw would play against the defending champion for the honor of taking home the Davis Cup trophy. The event started in 1900 and was the brainchild of another Harvard man, Dwight Davis.

Playing for the United States in the Davis Cup was a dream come true for Dick. There was a bit of controversy as to whether or not he could be on the team since he had lived almost all his life in Switzerland, but he was an American citizen after all, and in the end, he was allowed to be on the team. He was the second singles player right behind Mac. The two led the United States through a steamrolling of the Australasian team in a tie in New York earlier that month and were now headed to Britain for the rest of the competition. Davis Cup was a team sport and Dick found it really suited him. He loved being around the other players, helping each other out, spending time together, cheering each other on. Winning Wimbledon or the U.S. Nationals paled in comparison with the goal of bringing home the Davis Cup. Being part of the U.S. team was especially fun for Dick and he was determined not to let the pressure get to him, the highs or lows, the way it had the previous year.

He was surprised at how good he was feeling, how easy it had been to establish and maintain an enjoyable life in the past year. He was able to move on rather quickly from his devastating defeat to McLoughlin in the U.S. Nationals the previous year. Harvard was full of distractions, from the tennis team to studying, to an increasingly busy social life. He was feeling better about himself than he ever had. He still rarely thought about the *Titanic* and never talked about it. What was the point? The past was the past and he was going to only live in the present and prepare for the future, not dwell in the past. There was no way to change what had happened. He just had to keep living his life. This is what made him so frustrated with the nightmares — what was the point of his mind dwelling on something tragic that happened in the past? He had too many good things in his life to focus on.

He and Mac had struck up a rather unlikely friendship. His father always discouraged him from becoming friends with his rivals, thinking that it would make it harder to beat them on the court. But with Mac, he found it easy to separate their friendship from their tennis matches. Mac, who at twenty-three was only a year older than Dick, had a great sense of humor and was adept at traveling alone. A lot of the other tennis players always had their wife or parents with them, but Mac traveled alone, just like Dick. He was relaxed but lived life to the fullest, something that Dick really admired. They were excellent complements to one another — Dick loved to have fun on and off court, whereas Mac was a fighter and an extremely hard worker. Together they tended to bring out the best in each other.

Plus, right now they had a common goal – to bring the Davis Cup home to the United States for the first time in eleven years. This was their chance to be national heroes, to do something that would go down in history. They knew they had a great shot at making it happen. After all, McLoughlin was the U.S. national champion and was considered the favorite to make it through the all-comers' draw at Wimbledon and try to unseat New Zealand's Tony Wilding as champion. And Dick, the young phenom and second-best player in America, won both his matches against Australasia, although it was against the lesser-regarded Australasians Stanley Doust and Horace Rice.

Before the Davis Cup, however, came the British Championships at Wimbledon. Though they were known informally as the world championships of tennis, to most fans the tournament was still primarily a warmup for the Davis Cup final rounds. Wimbledon was a special place for Dick. He saw competitive tennis there for the first time at the All England Club at Worple Road outside of London when he was a youngster. He still remembered sitting on his father's shoulders at the outside courts as his father explained every intricacy of the game to him.

Still a bit groggy and unbalanced from the sea crossing, unused to the cold and damp London climate, and without his beloved spikes, which were illegal at Wimbledon, McLoughlin barely made it through a tough five-set opening-round match against Britain's Herbert Roper Barrett, a two-time Wimbledon finalist. Dick, in contrast, got a default in his first match from his opponent. After that, though, Mac steamrolled through the next three rounds, as did Dick, setting up a fourth-round match-up between the two American teammates. McLoughlin brought the British crowds to their feet with his mad-dashing serve-and-volley style, while Dick impressed with his powerful serve and backhand drives. But, before their match, Dick and Mac had a meeting with Harold Hackett, the playing captain of the U.S. Davis Cup captain.

"Boys," said Harold, "I received a wire from New York from the brass at the U.S. National Lawn Tennis Association and we can't have you beating each other up in a five-set marathon. That would leave the winner depleted for the rest of the tournament. Now, our best chance for an American champion is Mac, and so Dick, I want you to do the patriotic thing and do no more than give him a bit of practice. Your time will come. Don't worry."

Dick smiled. "I understand, Hal." And indeed he did. This was common practice in those days, as he well knew from his religious reading of *American Lawn Tennis* every fortnight. And so, when he and Mac walked out on court that bright warm day at the end of June, it felt more like a practice than a Wimbledon fourth-round battle. Strange practice, though, with the grandstand packed, the people oohing and aahing at every great shot. McLoughlin took the opportunity to practice his groundstrokes, forgoing his serve-and-volley attacks and staying back on the baseline. Dick, for his part, after giving his teammate a few deep shots to practice with, would usually end the point by going for some spectacular shot or other to please the crowd. Which it did: he earned more than his share of warm applause. And after he lost the first two sets 6-4, 6-4, the wild attempts started falling in. He blasted winner after winner, despite himself, and took the third set 6-3. But then he looked over to Hackett, who was watching from the front row. Hal was applauding but also giving Dick a meaningful look. Dick smiled, and as the players switched ends of the court, he walked up to McLoughlin and shook his hand.

"That's enough practice for you, Mac. Now that you see what I'm going to do to you next year, you'd better rest up for the next round."

McLoughlin laughed with him. "Thank you, my friend. And next time may I recommend that you play your matches with your eyes open? I'd like to see you hit those mad shots when the match is for real!"

Dick turned to the umpire. "Sir, I am retiring." They both shook hands with the umpire and walked off the court together. McLoughlin went on to become the first American to win the all-comers' draw, before losing a tough Challenge Round to the defender Wilding. Dick immediately turned his thoughts and preparations to the Cup.

Beginning a week after Wimbledon, with plenty of time to practice more on the English grass courts, the Americans absolutely breezed through their semifinal and final ties against Germany and Canada, with both Mac and Dick winning all of their singles matches. McLoughlin teamed with Hackett, who at thirty-five was still a great doubles specialist, to win both of their doubles matches. It was an unprecedented run for the United States team to dominate so thoroughly and they went in to the Challenge Round against the British team as favorites.

The Challenge Round took place at Wimbledon, as had the previous round against Canada, but now they would be up against the home team and the defending champions. They only had to win three matches, however, and McLoughlin alone was likely good for two of them. He opened up the tie playing the first match against James Parke, a solid English player with a good baseline game who clinched the Cup for the Brits in the decisive match the previous year in Melbourne against the Australasians.

Mac was a solid favorite to win, but the unthinkable happened — he lost. He got down early, had to win the fourth set to even things up, but then it seemed a sure thing once again. Even at five games all in the fifth, no one thought he would really lose. But then it was over 7-5 in the fifth set for Parke and the Americans were in grave of danger of failing in their quest. It was a stunning upset. Since Dick had been on the U.S. team, Mac had not lost a singles match. He was a fighter with impeccable tenacity and he could out-last anyone. Suddenly all the pressure was squarely on Dick's shoulders to beat Britain's best player or else they'd be down two matches to none, on the brink of defeat. It was one thing to feel the pressure he had put on himself last summer to win matches, but this was an entirely new kind of pressure. If he lost not only would he let himself down, but he'd let his teammates and his country down.

He was playing against Charles Dixon, a player who had won four Olympic medals in tennis whom his father had talked about often. However, he suddenly found himself unable to remember any of his father's words about him. Usually he was able to recall every word from those moleskin notebooks, as though he could see right to the bottom of the sea. After all, his father had read them to him over and over, so often. Usually he could even hear his father's voice while he was on the tennis court, reading him the notes. But here, in one of the biggest matches he had ever played, he found himself all alone, with only his own game to rely on.

He surprised even himself with his reaction, playing one of the most thrilling matches he had ever played. He won two out of the first three sets, but in the fourth set Dixon reached another level of tennis. In the blink of an eye, Dick lost that set 6-1 and the match went into a deciding fifth set. If only he could remember what his father had said about Dixon, if only thousands of British fans weren't cheering against him, if only he hadn't been having those nightmares, maybe then he'd have enough confidence and energy to pull out the match. Then he looked over at McLoughlin and Hackett, who were on their feet cheering for him, and he suddenly realized what a special opportunity he had. He had the opportunity to not only be a hero himself, but to let his friends be heroes. They believed that he could do this and they believed that they could do it. This was not the time to dwell on all the reasons he couldn't win. This was just the time to play tennis.

He locked eyes with Mac, who ruffled his own bright red hair, smiled and closed his eyes. Dick almost laughed out loud. Mac had always been so clean cut and hard-working and had a habit of taking things too seriously. When they were practicing for the tie against Australasia, he had been taking things so seriously and was working so hard, that one night after his fourth hour of practice, Dick went up to him and ruffled up his hair, saying "Hey, this is supposed to be fun!" And now Mac was reminding him of that, reminding him of his joke at the end of their fourth-round match at Wimbledon. *Play like your eyes are closed.*

With a smile on his face, Dick matched Dixon shot for shot in the fifth set, not going quite as much for broke as in that "practice" match, perhaps, but playing relaxed, aggressive tennis. At 6-5 in the fifth, a game away from winning the match and putting his team right back into winning position, Dick played some of the most aggressive tennis he had ever played, taking the balls on the rise and finding angles on his returns that left Dixon's head spinning. Dick pulled it out 7-5 in the fifth set, a win that he would always feel was one of the most important of his career, mainly because it was about so much more than him. Mac and Hackett took the momentum into the next day and won the doubles 6-4 in the fifth set against Dixon and Roper-Barrett to give the U.S. the pivotal 2-1 lead going into the final day's reverse singles. McLoughlin then sealed the trophy for the United States defeating Dixon in three sets on the final day of competition.

They were Davis Cup Champions.

After the victory, Dick invited Mac to go traveling around Europe with him for a few days. They both needed to relax and clear their heads, especially since when they got back to the United States, they would be only a week away from the Nationals. Plus, it was his first time in Europe since he had embarked at Cherbourg that fateful day. As anxious as he was about revisiting tragic memories, he had badly missed the milieu of his childhood. This was where he had grown up and he was feeling rather nostalgic for his former life.

It was fun to take Mac around, too. McLoughlin was an anomaly in the tennis community — he didn't grow up as a member of a very wealthy family playing tennis at elite country clubs. Rather, he learned how to play on the public courts in California and worked his way up to being the best player in the country. He had never traveled extensively in Europe before and it was fun to show him some of the most beautiful places in the world. In many ways, it helped Dick gain some perspective on his life, to once again realize how blessed he was and that he had much to be grateful for. They made sure to keep their tennis games finely tuned and sought out tennis courts in every town they visited.

At the end of their trip they were in Montreaux, a little town in the Swiss mountains that Dick and his father had visited several times. They were taking a walk after hitting some balls at the hotel, a rather strenuous hike, actually, on a gorgeous mountaintop, when they stumbled upon an enclave of red clay tennis courts. The setting was beginning to feel rather familiar when he heard a man call his name — it turned out they were at the location of a well-known interclub tournament that Dick had completely forgotten about. In fact, the tournament was about to commence!

All the players and officials at the club were thrilled to see him and he was shocked to find out that not only did they remember him and his father very well, but they had all been following his success in America. His picture with the trophy — from when he was sixteen — was displayed prominently on the wall in the entrance of the clubhouse. They had also saved newspaper clippings from all of his triumphs in the U.S. It was a humbling thing to see since he'd lost his father. He had always imagined that there was nobody really following what he did closely, that all those people who knew his father just remembered him and that their memories of Dick would fade away. He was so quiet and reserved back then, so much in the shadow of his father. It was comforting but also a bit alarming — he had people to please, even when he wasn't playing Davis Cup. This wasn't just about him. It was about preserving his father's memory and making sure that he did them proud.

When Mac was out of sight, the locals would whisper to him, "We'll be rooting for you at the U.S. Nationals. This is your year." He thought back to last year, when he had believed the very same thing, when he had told himself those very same lies. It was bewildering to Dick to have people from far-away places following his results and career, rooting for him. In many ways, it made him want to win in Newport even more. He wanted to win the title for himself, for his father, and now for these people too.

Nevertheless, later that month, just a few days off the boat, he went into the 1913 Nationals at Newport hoping that it was true, believing that it was his year and that he could earn that trophy. He knew what he was doing this year. Nothing was a surprise to him. He was a stronger player, more used to his public profile and a better man than he had been a year ago. He could close his eyes and see himself holding that trophy. He could feel the waves of closure flowing through his body, making everything worth it.

He had a close match against Gustave Touchard in the second round that almost cost him an early exit from the tournament, but just like in the Davis Cup match against Dixon, he was able to dig deep and take the fifth set 7-5. It didn't hurt that when Touchard was serving at 4-3, 40-30 in the final set he was called for a foot fault, after which, rattled, he double faulted and then really blew his stack. Still, for Dick a victory was a victory. He was sure he could carry the momentum to win the title.

Aside from a close four-setter in the fourth round against William Johnston, the Californian with the big Western topspin forehand, Dick had an easy time after Touchard, making it all the way to the final, where of course his new friend and teammate Maurice McLoughlin waited for him. Mac was trying to win the title for the second year in a row and continue his run as the best player in the country. For Dick, the championship had special symbolic value. He yearned to finish the journey he started sixteen months earlier when he boarded the *Titanic* with his father.

After having played against each other almost every day for the past three months, both players knew each others' game as well as their own. Dick was able to handle the forceful serves of his Davis Cup teammate like no one else and often dictated play off his own racket. After losing a hard-fought first set 6-4, Dick continued his aggressive play and was able to steal the second set 7-5 – becoming the first player to secure a set from Mac at the tournament. The tennis was some of the most dazzling play that the Newport fans had ever seen. After some tense play early in the third set, the match was up for grabs. As the crowd grew louder and louder after every point and they started to move in between points, leaning on the edge of their seats to see every shot, Dick started to struggle. He tried to focus in, to block the world out with his tennis like he had been doing for the past year and a half, but it wasn't working. The clapping began to sound like the ship breaking into two. Cheers sounded like cries. The memories he was trying so hard to block out came crashing down on him at one of the worst times possible. Mac took control of the match mid-way through the third set and eased to a four-set victory 6-4, 5-7, 6-3, 6-1. "The California Comet" had another trophy for his shelf and Dick had to wait another year for another chance.

Karl snuck into his apartment quietly. It was after midnight and he didn't want to wake Helen. He was having trouble sleeping again due to recurring nightmares, but he found if he got up and went for a quiet walk, or read the papers, that he was able to fall asleep much easier. He walked over to his desk and sat down to get caught up on his reading.

It had been a wonderful but exhausting summer for Karl and Helen. After the wedding, they went off on an extended honeymoon and since coming back, he was overwhelmed with responsibility at his father's company. He had recently been named the president, a testament both to his hard work over the years and the fact that his father's health was rapidly fading. The hours and travel had been an adjustment for both him and Helen, but it was good to stay busy.

He perused a stack of papers he'd set aside, most of them recaps of what was going on in tennis. He missed the game a lot. He hadn't had any time that summer to compete and wondered if he would ever play competitively again. As it seemed was always the case recently, all of the tennis articles he came across were mostly about Dick. Helen and her family kept a close eye on all of Dick's accomplishments, saving all the newspaper clippings and sending them to Karl, certain that he'd be thrilled for his friend's accomplishments. But for Karl, it was hard. He felt like he was missing out. It was especially tough to read about Dick's Davis Cup successes – Karl had only played on a Davis Cup team once, in a losing effort to Australasia in 1907 – yet he had always hoped to get a chance to play on the team again. Now here was young Dick already the number two American, reaching the Newport final and giving McLoughlin a run for his money, while Karl was busy with work and family, unable to play. He'd even quixotically sent in his application to the Nationals, but when the time came, and he hadn't had time to practice and get in shape, he did not show and defaulted his first-round match.

He was startled when he heard Helen get out of bed and he quickly tried to hide the clippings, as well as his sad mood, before she saw them. It was too late though. She sat on his lap and put her arms around him. He kissed her on the temple.

"You should play again, Karl. I know you miss it."

"Things are just too busy at work. You know that."

"You're the boss now, though. You could get someone else to do the traveling, at least for next summer."

He knew she was right. There was no good excuse not to

get back out there if it was what he really wanted to do. He felt he had a lot of tennis left in him and a lot to prove to the world. He had always been so distracted. He used to dream of winning the Nationals, of winning the Davis Cup for the United States. Somewhere along the line he lost that fire and determination. He wondered if it was possible to get it back.

"Besides, Karl, I know of someone who would love to see their father play." She motioned to her stomach, a giant smile taking over her face.

They were going to have a baby.

22

The summer of 1914 was full of tension. In late June, the Austrian Archduke Franz Ferdinand's murder set off a chain reaction of hostility in Europe between Austria-Hungary, Serbia, Russia, Germany and France that ignited a world war. When Britain became involved in the conflict on August 4, formally declaring war on Germany, it seemed improbable that the United States would be able to maintain its declaration of neutrality. As young men in Europe were thrown into battle, American men were still going about their daily lives, unsure if and when they might be called into action.

With one eye on the war, and despite his continued responsibilities at work and at home with Helen and their new baby, Karl, Jr., Karl Behr was managing to fulfill his promise to himself and was in the midst of one of the best tennis years of his life at the age of twenty-nine. He started out the season beating Alexander Pell and Gustave Touchard, two of the top players in the country, in the final and challenge round at the Middle States Championships to win his first title in six years. He was also feeling a lot of support from his peers as he successfully led a petition to get the U.S. Nationals moved from the coastal enclave of Newport, Rhode Island to a larger metropolitan venue at the West Side Tennis Club in Forest Hills, New York, a move he felt was important for the future growth of the sport.

The popularity of tennis was at an all-time high – players from all across the country were traveling for months on end competing in tournaments. Fan attendance swelled, indicating the increased popularity of the sport. There were exponentially more tournaments in 1914 than when Karl was starting out. The U.S. Nationals were growing in prestige as more top players from overseas began to come over more frequently. Even within the United States, there were many more players from California and other parts of the country competing in events, further threatening the east coast domination of the sport. Universities were putting more emphasis and focus on tennis programs and Karl knew enough about business and fundraising to know that a small Rhode Island town could no longer keep up with the growing demands of the sport.

The 1914 U.S. Nationals was the final year the event was going to be staged at the Newport Casino. To top it all off, Karl had enough good wins over the summer to secure a spot on the U.S. Davis Cup team for the first time since 1907. This represented the achievement of an enormous goal for him; he had always wanted an opportunity to redeem himself for his country. And nothing made his father prouder than when he played on the Davis Cup team.

The United States was the defending Cup champion, thanks to the efforts of Dick, as well as Maurice McLoughlin in Britain the previous year, and therefore they would be hosting the Challenge Round. The West Side Tennis Club was selected as the site for the matches, to be played in early August, just prior to the U.S. Nationals. The Australasian team, led by four-time defending Wimbledon champion Tony Wilding of New Zealand and Australian legend Norman Brookes, emerged as the challengers to the United States.

Karl was realistic enough to know that he wouldn't be picked for singles, as Dick and Mac clearly had those spots locked up, but he hoped he might get to play the doubles. He won quite a few doubles titles in his career, was the doubles runner-up at Wimbledon in 1907, and had the experience of beating Brookes and Wilding before in doubles. Now, playing the tennis of his life, he was hopeful for his chances. With his child being born and his father down to his final years, he wanted to seize any opportunity he had to make them proud.

But the Davis Cup, which promised to be the crowning moment in Karl's career, turned into bitter disappointment. To begin with, it marked the first time since the *Carpathia* that he and Dick spent any significant amount of time together. They had great team camaraderie and experienced good times, but there was still an *awkwardness* the pervaded. They were not able to talk like they had on the *Carpathia* — the team environment not conducive for long, one-on-one in-depth talks. Karl was also surprised at how uncomfortable he felt as the U.S. team clearly belonged to Dick and Mac. They won the trophy the year before in dominant fashion, were the best two players in the country for two straight years, and more than that, the two had formed a good friendship that made Karl feel even more like an outsider.

Karl seemed poised to be selected to play the doubles with McLoughlin as his consistency seemed to mix well with the brilliant but sometimes reckless shot-making abilities of "the California Comet". McLoughlin was the reigning U.S. doubles champion with another Californian, Tom Bundy, but Bundy was not in top form and was not as fast on the court as in previous years.

Karl made a strong statement for selection to the team when he and a fellow American standout Ted Pell actually beat McLoughlin and Bundy 6-2, 6-3 in a practice match to help determine the team. "It would be a crime to leave Behr off the doubles team in the Davis Cup matches," one top player even anonymously told the papers. But then Karl played a bad match — one bad match! — in the doubles semifinals of a tournament in Chicago, when he and Pell lost to a relatively unheralded team of G.M. Church and Dean Mathey from Princeton University and suddenly everyone was whispering that they'd better keep Mac with his old partner Bundy.

And that's what happened. Karl was relegated to cheerleader status on the team. The U.S. Davis Cup Committee waited until the last minute to announce the doubles team, so late that Karl's father, in his fragile health, went all the way out to Forest Hills only to watch his son sit on the bench.

For his part, Dick didn't seem to be having a good week at Forest Hills. He seemed different to Karl. While he had transformed from a shy and inexperienced kid on the *Carpathia* into a confident and established tennis star, comfortable charming the crowds and being in the spotlight, he now seemed a bit more volatile. He put on a good show and continued to be as social as he had been, but it looked to Karl like the pressure was finally getting to him. It must be tough to win so much, Karl would think to himself sarcastically, unable to sympathize with the man who had so instantly jumped to heights of success that was not able to reach.

Karl would love to have had the pressure of playing Davis Cup matches, but against Australasia it seemed like Dick was out of sorts, seemingly unable to handle the hype, pressure and spectacle that the Davis Cup Challenge Round created. He would play a beautiful shot followed by some of the most silly and aggressive shots, and seemed to be walking around in a bit of a fog. He lacked consistency, making many errors and served with reckless abandon, hitting first and second serves with the same pace, causing many double faults.

Dick did not lose a singles match that counted in the entire Davis Cup competition in 1913, but against Australasia at Forest Hills, he lost to both Brookes and Wilding, unable to carry his weight and succumbing to the pressure and the fine play of his adversaries. In the opening match of the series, which was witnessed by a crowd of 13,000, the largest crowd to ever watch a tennis match, Dick was man-handled by Wilding 7-5, 6-2, 6-3. His four-set loss to Brookes on the third day of play clinched the Cup for the Australasians. Dick was not able to ascend to the heights of playing for his country as he did the previous year against the British team at Wimbledon.

As much as Karl was hoping for his country to retain the Cup, he couldn't help but feel a modicum of vindication when McLoughlin and Bundy played one of the poorest exhibitions of Davis Cup doubles that reporters remembered, losing to Brookes and Wilding in three straight sets. That, combined with Dick's lusterless performances, was what allowed the Cup to slip from the Americans grasp. And with war now raging in Europe – Brookes and Wilding set sail immediately after the matches for Britain to join their regiments as part of the British Commonwealth – one had to even wonder when there would next be a Davis Cup competition.

McLoughlin, however, did provide one great highlight during the series. On the first day, after Dick lost meekly to Wilding, McLoughlin and Brookes played the most sensational set of tennis that he, or anyone for that matter, had ever seen. The set was an entire match in itself featuring more games than any set in the history of the sport. McLoughlin was able to win it 17-15 on the strength of his famous cannonball serve and trademark grit and determination.

It was truly a time when Karl felt lucky just to be there on the team, just to be witnessing such a feat of physical endurance. He sat on the U.S. team bench, a sea of straw hats undulating right and left all around him, experiencing the greatest occasion yet in his sport's history. It made Karl want to be a better player and a better man. Sometimes matches could do that to you. It was the marvelous thing about sports. Though the United States lost the Cup and he did not get a chance to play, Karl came away from the experience inspired to finish the season strong at Newport. He wanted to dig deep, make up for the slight at not being selected to play and show the kind of fight that Mac had, to be able to last to 17-15, or even longer, to win a set, if that was truly what it took.

Even when he was awake, anything could trigger it, at any moment – a dog's bark, the slam of a book or the creak of a grandstand when he was in the middle of a match. Sometimes even applause, the happiest of sounds, would remind Dick of the sound of the ship as it sank. Nightmares of the *Titanic* horror became more frequent. The memory jolts, as he called them to himself, started coming to him on the ship to England the previous summer with the Davis Cup team. They gradually increased in frequency throughout the year. He feared that people would think he was going crazy, so he overcompensated by keeping himself busy and surrounded by others at all times. He was really just wearing himself thin and he knew it. It was becoming harder and harder to pretend that everything was all right. He maintained a façade of well being for the most part, though, excelling at Harvard during both sessions and throwing himself into tennis once again over the summer. But the pressures of school, life and of the Davis Cup and the U.S. Nationals escalated. He was exhausted.

After the Davis Cup debacle, Dick's confidence was shattered and winning anything seemed improbable. In front of the largest crowed to ever watch tennis, and playing for his country, he was unable to rise to the occasion. He tried to block out the crowd, but every sound emanating from the stands brought him back to the sinking ship and the bone-freezing sea. It was almost a post-traumatic stress episode where the pressures of the present were combined with the anxieties of the past. Dick tried to dig deep and find his game, but it just wouldn't work. Brookes and Wilding were too talented to face if he wasn't at his best. Despite winning three tournaments already that year, he had to wonder if he was even capable of playing at Newport without completely humiliating himself.

In addition, Dick was unhappy by the decision to move the Nationals from their historic home at the Newport Casino and he knew his father would be disappointed that he'd been unable to dissuade the U.S. National Lawn Tennis Association in their decision. His father loved Newport and Dick grew up listening to stories of some of the great players and matches played on its lawns. His father was a creature of tradition and fell in love with the sport on the Casino's grass. Dick was upset that he couldn't stand up for them. He offered no convincing rebuttal to the proposal, supported by Karl, to move the tournament to New York City. This failure put more pressure on him, in his own mind, to win the Nationals in this final year at Newport. It was another way to pay homage to his father.

On his way from New York to Newport he stopped by his mother's house outside Boston for a few days for a rest and visit. During the school year, he made sure to stop by once a week to get her groceries and have lunch. Just like in Geneva, she didn't leave the house often but he enjoyed their weekly visits. He had to admit that it felt good to have her close by. She didn't come to his matches as it made her too nervous but she always kept track of when and where he was playing.

He had not seen her all summer long and was looking forward to getting an opportunity to clear his head a little before the pressure of the upcoming national championships completely swallowed him up. However, even at her house he found himself agitated and unable to sleep, taking it out on her more than he did on anyone else. It was always like that with family. When truly comfortable around someone you could let them see you at your worst and nobody else in his life now had that sort of unconditional love for him. Still, he knew he should be treating her better.

They were having lunch one of the first days of his visit – tomato sandwiches like they always had during the summer – and sat in silence like they usually did. Normally the silence between them was comforting and natural, but because of the way he had been behaving over the last few days it felt tense.

"Dick, I want to show you something your father sent me."

This was more than he could handle. His brain was foggy. He was upset at himself for how he had spoken to her earlier. It certainly didn't seem like the right moment for them to talk about his father.

He recognized the postcard immediately – it was from Zurich, Switzerland where he played his very first tennis tournament. He was only twelve years old but Charles was convinced that he could compete just fine with the older boys, so he was entered into the fifteen-year-old division. He was never a big guy, even now at twenty-three, but at twelve he only came up to the chests of the older boys playing in the tournament. In his first match, he was drawn against one of the top seeds in the tournament and lost 6-2, 4-6, 6-0. Dick was so embarrassed about the loss and felt like such a disappointment that he considered not playing tournaments again.

"Read what your father wrote on the back."

> *You would be so proud of our son. He gave it his all out there against a boy twice his size. I don't think I could ever be prouder of him than I am at this very moment.*
>
> *Love, Charles*

"I know your father was always pushing you toward enormous goals, but he was proud of you no matter what. He would just want you to be happy."

For some reason, though these were some of the last words his father said to him, he didn't remember them until just now.

23

Karl lingered outside the locker room at the Newport Casino for as long as possible. He was about to go in to get ready for his biggest match in seven years – the quarterfinals of the 1914 U.S. Nationals – but he couldn't bring himself to say goodbye to Helen and Karl, Jr.

Karl, Jr. was eight months old and had Helen's eyes, her smile and her perfect nose. Like most men, Karl was unprepared for becoming a father in so many ways, underestimating the time and financial commitments – not to mention the lack of sleep – but he loved every moment of parenthood and being with his son.

Helen was a model of grace throughout the pregnancy, never complaining at all. Although she supported and believed that women should have a right to go to work, she was perfectly happy since the birth to stay at home with Karl, Jr. and let Karl focus on his father's growing company and tennis at the same time. She was completely selfless. The birth of their son brought them together even closer, if that was possible. At home, he was living the life he had dreamed about. Now, it was time to say goodbye and prepare mentally to try and accomplish another dream.

"You ready to watch daddy play a tennis match? Are you?" Helen cooed in her new maternal voice.

"I'm going to win this one just for you, son," Karl said in a mock serious tone, as he kissed his baby on his forehead and Helen on the lips.

"Good luck," she said with a smile as she left to find Gertie, Frederich, Max and her parents and take their places in the stands. Three of his siblings, his wife and son, and his in-laws were all in Newport to see the match on the main grandstand court in front of almost four thousand of the finest members of society.

He came into the tournament with extra confidence in his chances and breezed through the first two rounds, losing only seven games in the process. After a one-set hiccup in his third-round match against Robert LeRoy, he ran into a talented young twenty-one-year-old left-hander from Palo Alto, California, Lindley Murray, where Karl was the decided underdog. The two men engaged in a physical, exhaustive battle as each player traded blows against each other as if they were boxers. On this day, the older man would carry the day – Karl winning a 3-6, 6-2, 7-5, 3-6, 8-6 decision.

The quarterfinals, however, were different.

In the quarterfinals, he was playing Dick.

It was hard to comprehend that two men who survived the sinking of the *Titanic*, who met on the deck of the *Carpathia* among so much sorrow and tragedy, would meet on such a big stage on the courts of Newport to determine which man would continue on the route to the U.S. National tennis title.

Karl was riding a wave of confidence from his victory over the talented youngster Murray, and he had witnessed up close in Forest Hills how erratic Dick's tennis had the potential to be. It was going to be a special day. He could feel it.

Karl entered the locker room cautiously, only to find his fears confirmed — it was just he and Dick alone in the room. All of the other matches were out on court or already finished for the day. Dick was fiddling with his rackets, checking string tension as he had a habit of doing until the very last minute, looking nervous and antsy, not at all like the second best player in the country should look before such a big match.

Karl went to his locker, about seven spots away from Dick's, in the right corner of the room, still a bit too close for comfort. When he opened his locker the mirror inside presented an image of Dick, and as Karl positioned his headband just so and fixed his glasses so they wouldn't fall off during play, he watched his opponent tie his shoes three times in a row, each time seemingly disgusted with the result. Dick checked his racket tension again, tied his shoes again, jogged in place, and then repeated the whole routine. Mesmerizing – it could be the routine a champion or a madman. Perhaps the dark secret was that there wasn't that much of a difference between the two.

Karl slammed his locker, checked his racket tension only once – he always carried four rackets out with him and always strung them himself, the exact same way. He never fretted over things like that. Equipment didn't lose matches – people did. Other players obsessed over the type and quality of balls, the size and tension of their racket and the make and model of their shoes as if they were all parts to a car, and if one of them was off a bit, the whole thing would fall apart. He didn't believe in any of that. The key to the game was between the ears and a champion could win with any racket.

"Mr. Behr and Mr. Williams: two minutes."

Karl stretched his legs a little bit, rolled his neck and made sure his headband was secure. A tournament steward came in and escorted the players out of the locker room, down the path between the practice courts and between the grandstands to the court. Karl kept his head down, concentrating on his steps, but he could hear the crowd react to the appearance of the two players. He heard a baby's cry and was glad to note that it wasn't his son. The crowd rose to their feet as he and Dick entered the court and while he knew they were probably more excited to see Dick, he was thrilled nonetheless. He found his family in the stands and smiled at them, before closing his eyes to block it all out, taking a deep breath and walking out to his side of the court. He looked up at Dick, standing on the opposite side of the net with seventy-eight feet of grass separating them, and nodded. Karl took one of the new white balls from his hand and gave it the familiar, comforting blow of force from his racket to start the pre-match warmup. After all, it was just tennis.

Karl was completely focused in the warmup. He was moving well, serving well and had a perfect feel for the court. He won the coin toss and elected to serve first, hoping to gain an edge early. He was able to do that. He held comfortably to start out the match, maintaining a steady mix of aggressive shots and forcing mistakes from Dick by moving him forcibly around the court. He knew that his best chance to beat Dick was to engage in a physical match, similar to their encounter at Longwood from 1912 and the one he played the day before against the young Murray. Dick liked to take the racket out of his opponents hand by taking risks and hitting daring shots. He knew if he gave him any time at all to set up shots, he would lose the match quickly. His best shot to win the match was to hit the ball hard and beat him at his own game.

After his first service game, Karl felt in control and confident. The late-afternoon crowd was subdued after being in the heat all day, but they would certainly get behind him as the underdog, he felt.

Dick's first service game also went by in a flash. His serves were powerful and difficult for Karl to return.

Karl's second service game didn't go as well as the first. He was rattled by Dick's precision and pace and it seemed that it only took Dick one game to groove his return of serve. He dug deep, upset that he was having to pull out his best serves so early in the match. But when they all came flying back at him — some as service-return winners — he was disheartened. Dick broke him with ease and Karl knew he had to fight hard and not lose his composure. He wasn't playing poorly, Dick was just playing on another level than Karl had seen. He had to keep his head up, fight hard and be patient. Karl was in for a battle, that was for sure.

Karl just couldn't seem to be able to predict where Dick's serves were going to go. When he sensed Dick was about to hit the serve down the middle, he would knock it wide to the corner. If he anticipated the ball coming to his forehand, it would go to his backhand. There was a crispness and purposeful deception to Dick's shots that wasn't there previously.

"Slow, steady and careful," Karl said to himself, just like Gertie had told him so many years ago. Unfortunately, there wasn't anything "slow" about this match.

Karl dropped the first set 6-1 before he even had a chance to finish talking to himself about composure and focus. As they changed ends, he took an extra long drink and fiddled with his equipment, trying to steady himself. He lost the first set against Murray too, and still managed to win that match.

Just keep fighting. He thought about McLoughlin, about that 17-15 set at Forest Hills in the Davis Cup. He remembered that anything was possible. He looked over at his family and thought of his father who was unable to travel to Newport due to his health. This match was far from over.

Even after Dick secured the second set by a 6-2 margin, Karl kept his composure. He still truly felt that he could crawl back into the match like he had done against Dick in their match at Longwood back two years earlier. He could do it again and come back from two sets down and beat Dick just as he had done in handing him his first-ever loss in America. There was no way Dick could keep up this level of play for another set. His hot hand had to cool at some point. Karl really dug his heels in the third set, sensing that Dick might get overconfident and perhaps lose some concentration by trying some flashy, low percentage shots and give him a small window to secure a service break.

At 3-3 in the third set, Dick unexpectedly threw in a double fault and Karl was able to get the score to deuce. The crowd, lulled into complacency by Dick's routine ease of winning, started to stir a bit. Karl could hear Helen, Gertie and Max cheering him on from the grandstand. This was it. This was the opening he was waiting for. He just needed two more points for the break and he could be on his way out of this hole.

But Dick responded by hitting two unreturnable serves. Any chance of breaking serve seemed like a far off hope. There was a sense of inevitability to the rest of the match, even though Karl managed to stay on serve for a few more games. At 5-5, though, he was suddenly aware of just how exhausted he was from the marathon he played the day before. Dick held easily, then broke Karl in the final game with return winners that made it seem he could conjure them on command. It was over – 6-1, 6-2, 7-5.

All losses hurt for Karl, but this was different. It wasn't that he played poorly or that there had been any mental lapses. He simply wasn't good enough. More than that, Dick was just too strong and was the better player. As he looked over at his eight-month-old son in the stands he thought, this was going to be a tough lesson to pass on. Sometimes you're just not good enough.

The finality of the defeat, and the loss of his tennis hopes for the year, washed over Karl. The match did not even last ninety minutes. Across the net, Dick flashed his trademark grin and blushed a bit, almost in embarrassment at how easy it had been. For the first time in two years, Karl recognized the face of the boy lying on the deck of the *Carpathia*. He remembered the doctor telling Dick that his legs needed to be amputated and Dick's impassioned pleas and efforts to preserve them. He remembered helping Dick walk through the excruciating pain across the ship's deck among so much other suffering and misery. He was suddenly able to reconcile that boy from the *Carpathia* with the man who had just beaten him.

The two men shook hands at the net and Karl put his arm around Dick, much the way he had when he had helped the boy to his feet to save his legs two years ago.

"I should have let them amputate your legs," he said with a smile, and though the younger man's head was hanging down and the applause rained down from the bleachers, Karl could hear and feel Dick laughing with him as they walked, arms around each other's shoulders, off the court.

24

Dick stood next to his locker, practically using the door to keep him standing upright. The matches were over for the day, but he stayed around long after everyone else was gone. His semifinal was scheduled for the next morning and in that situation he liked to make sure his equipment was in order in advance. Of course, he knew that he'd fuss with everything in the morning anyway.

The match with Karl was a lot easier than he expected. He was happy both with his mental ability to keep out thoughts of the past and with how his game seemed to be finally clicking after the disastrous Davis Cup. Still, he was tired – mentally and physically. He was relieved that the ordeal of playing Karl was over, but his feelings were conflicted. He was thrilled of course to be through to the semifinals and he was glad that he had been able to conserve his energy and get the win with very little effort, but he also found himself feeling guilty. It was though he wished there was a way where they could both win.

He caught a glimpse of himself in the mirror and was taken aback by how much he looked like his father. He stood there, propped up against the locker and stared at his reflection. How was it possible that didn't notice this before? He most certainly had his father's eyes. He wondered what his father was like at his age. He was already a top lawyer and married. Here was Dick, one of the top American tennis players and a top contender to win the U.S. Nationals. It was just as his father wanted. It was now what he wanted.

He thought about the gift his mother gave him by showing him the postcard from Zurich, and about how his father's final message to him was about being happy. Tennis made him feel closer to his father, that was for sure. It gave his life structure. It gave him opportunities he would not have had otherwise.

He remembered how motivated he was to go to Harvard and study everything under the sun, but his social involvement and tennis had prevented him from exploring as much as he would like. He was going to join clubs, study history, become somewhat of a scholar just like Harry Widener. He thought a lot about Major Butt now that the war started, wondering if there would ever come a time when he would go fight for his country. Three men, so passionate about their lives, had all gone down with the *Titanic*. He wanted to make them proud.

"Congratulations." Mac McLoughlin, thankfully, interrupted his reverie with a tap on the shoulder. Dick stood up, realizing suddenly that he needed to go at least try and get a good night of sleep before his semifinal match. He was playing a surprise semifinalist, Elia Fottrell, whom he didn't know much about, and was going to have to read about that night in the papers.

"Are you all right?" Mac looked concerned. Dick wondered if he looked as exhausted and confused as he felt.

"Yes, I'm fine, just tired."

"Are you still not sleeping?" They had roomed together so many times that Mac was well aware of his friend's night distresses, though he had never asked questions.

"I'm fine." Dick's yawn gave him away, though. He hated that he was showing any weakness or tension. After all, Mac could very well be his opponent at week's end for the championship.

He heard a door slam and wondered if anyone had overheard their conversation. He thanked Mac, wished him best of luck as well, and quickly showered, got dressed, and went out to the lobby. He was hoping to get to bed while he was still so exhausted and before his brain could convince him otherwise. Then, he heard a strangely familiar voice yell from across the Newport Casino lobby. It was Sallie Beckwith beckoning for him to come over. She was sitting with her husband, Helen, the baby and Karl around an enclave of couches by the fireplace.

She flung her arms around him and squeezed him uncomfortably tight.

"Oh Dick, it is so good to see you. It has just been too long! We ask Karl about you all the time."

He looked over to Karl, who was holding his son. Dick could so vividly remember that night in the thunderstorm on the *Carpathia* when he talked about how much he loved Helen and how much he wanted to have a family with her. He was sure that Karl was a great father.

"How have you been, son?" Richard asked. How was he even supposed to answer that?

"I've been fine, sir. How are you all?"

"Fine, just fine. Enjoying our new addition over there."

There was a pause, as if everyone else had just realized how awkward this was. He couldn't help but think about the last time they were all together, as they walked down that ramp into a crowd of forty thousand emotion-wracked New Yorkers. He wondered if everyone was thinking about the same thing. He looked up and realized that they were in fact staring at Karl, Jr., who was grabbing onto Karl's collar and biting it like it was a toy.

"I have to get back to my room to rest up for tomorrow," he hoped this didn't rankle Karl, but the new father seemed completely happy to be with his wife and baby. "But it was wonderful to see you all." He was surprised by how calm and collected he sounded, almost as if it were true.

"Good luck tomorrow, Dick," Sallie said with apparent sincerity. He had just beaten her son-in-law pretty soundly, but she was nothing if not proper, and, in fact, there was warmth in her voice. "We're proud of you. We're all survivors, you know."

Karl couldn't sleep that night. He thought about the fact that this might have been his last time playing at the Nationals. He thought about how many things were happening in his own life and in the world. He wondered if he had blown his last chance at winning that trophy. He thought about how well Dick played, about how innocent he looked afterwards and in the locker room. He heard him talking to Mac about the trouble he was having sleeping and remembered his own problems sleeping after the tragedy. Perhaps Dick hadn't brushed the *Titanic* into history quite as brashly as it had seemed.

Junior started crying in the bassinet next to them in their room and as Helen began to wake up, Karl told her to go back to sleep. He walked over and picked up his child, holding him tight in his arms. As disappointed as he was about his match with Dick, he gave it his best shot. He played as well as he possibly could.

Helen sat up in bed, staring at him and smiling. She had

often boasted that there was nothing more beautiful than seeing her husband hold their child.

"It was really good to see Dick today."

"I saw more of him than I would have preferred," Dick laughed.

"Oh come on Karl, you know what I mean. I worry about him. He's all alone."

Though the statement sounded ridiculous at first, as Dick was one of the most popular tennis players both amongst his peers and with the fans, he knew that there was some truth to it. Here he was, with his adoring wife and child. This was everything he had dreamed of before he stepped foot on the *Titanic*. At the end of the day, with or without championships at the U.S. Nationals or in Davis Cup, he had what he always wanted – Helen as his wife and the mother of his child. They were more important to him than any triumph on a tennis court. He could get through anything in life with them. He would get through anything *for* them. It was hard to imagine what it must have been like for Dick to go through the last two years without that. Karl and Helen had each other, their own unique support group having gone through the tragedy together. They were mutually cathartic to each other. And now he was a father. He wanted his son to be proud of him, but he knew that had little to do with a tennis match. Perhaps Dick was still in need of closure. Karl was going to find out.

25

Dick easily took care of his semifinal opponent Elia Fottrell in three quick sets and, for the third consecutive year, found himself up against Maurice McLoughlin in Newport – the second straight year in the final. Two years ago in the quarterfinals, he stretched Mac to five tough sets and seemed poised to take over the role of top American. But then in last year's final, Mac dismantled him in four sets and the dream of winning the Newport crown for his father was receding. With war raging and many calling for America to enter the fray, this could be his last chance to do it. Who knew? It could be the last chance for all of them.

He was rather shocked to see Karl Behr, in his tennis clothes, sitting in the locker room after the semifinals. Although it was still rather early in the day, it seemed a bit odd for him to be there for a practice the day after he was eliminated.

"Hello, Dick," said Karl.

"Hi there. Is everything all right?" He wondered if something had happened to Sallie or Richard.

"Oh, yes, everything's fine. I just wanted to see if, perhaps, you needed a practice partner to warm up with tomorrow before the final?"

Dick was confused. It was not typical for fellows to offer to warm up the man who had just knocked them out of the tournament. And as much as he wanted to go find somewhere to lie down, he was curious as to the real reason Karl was here. Could this be about the Forest Hills thing? Maybe he was going to apologize, maybe he had changed his mind and realized what a huge mistake it would be to move the Nationals from Newport?

"Sure, that would be a big help. Shall we meet here around ten tomorrow?"

The next morning, Karl and Dick quietly walked onto the most remote practice court, off in the southeast corner. They began knocking balls about the grass, in a leisurely manner at first, allowing Dick's limbs to loosen up gradually. After a while, they both began taking practice serves. "After my serve, Mac's will seem like a powder puff!" Karl shouted, both men immediately erupting into laughter.

"Oh yeah? Let's see your cannonball, then!" Dick shouted across the net, prompting Karl to launch into his best McLoughlin impression. Never mind that Mac was warming up himself over on the next row of courts with Wallace Johnson. Dick was transported right back to the Avantes Lawn and Tennis Club in Geneva, where he grew up, when his father was training him to learn how to return McLoughlin's serve by standing only halfway to the baseline.

Karl's impression was much closer to the real thing, as his own serve had a similar style and power to McLoughlin's. He didn't have quite the same mastery of deception, though. When you were playing Mac you always felt like you were leaning the wrong way, guessing the wrong corner. And if you did get it back, there he'd be, already at the net to knock off an easy volley winner. Still, he couldn't ask for a better warmup than this. Thinking back to the Geneva mountainside, he could suddenly hear his father's voice: "Take it early, Richard Norris! Take it early! Cut off the angle!"

"Give me another one," Dick shouted over to Karl, who seemed to be enjoying himself. He stretched as high as he could, caught the ball at its very apex and launched just about the best cannonball serve anyone other than Mac had ever hit. Dick stepped forward inside the baseline and took a short, truncated swing at the ball almost directly after it hit the ground. He was able to transfer the power swiftly back over the net right down the line. It happened so quickly Karl didn't even get a racket on the return.

"Now that's a return, Dick!"

"Do you think it will work today?"

"I think it's your best shot, Dick. If you can neutralize his serve so he's not coming from a position of power the entire match, then he's going to be more tentative with the rest of his game. If you then can get your first serve percentage up, so that you're doing to him what you did to me the other day, I think you should be fine."

It was great advice. It had been a while since he had heard any good guidance. They spent the next thirty minutes on court experimenting with just the serve and the return, making sure that he didn't get too worn out, but also laughing a lot.

As they were gathering their equipment it occurred to Dick that he still didn't know why Karl had rendered him this odd invitation to practice — he couldn't imagine that it had really just been to help him read Mac's serve, though he surely appreciated the advice.

"Is there anything else?" he asked as he picked up the last of their practice balls.

"Yes," Karl said, straightening up with rackets in hand. He cleared his throat and looked Dick directly in the eye. "I had trouble sleeping too. Nightmares."

Dick tensed up. He didn't know what to say. This was the last thing he had expected to hear from Karl. He looked down at the ground and bounced a tennis ball in his hand, before daring to make eye contact again.

"You did?"

"When we first got back, I had nightmares all the time. I couldn't stop myself from thinking about that night. It was crippling to be so traumatized day after day after day."

Dick internalized and compartmentalized the trauma from the horrific night when the *Titanic* sank. He put it in his past and rarely spoke about it all, even to his mother. It felt strange to have a conversation about it, but he knew he could talk to Karl since he was one of the few people in the world who could understand and relate to how he was feeling inside. Dick sat down on a chair next to their court. Karl sat down beside him.

"What did you do? How did you make them stop?" Dick asked sincerely.

"I finally started talking about it. I talked with Helen, sometimes Sallie and Richard too. I realized that what I was feeling was normal, that I wasn't alone. I was lucky to have a support system. I discovered that the only way to exorcise and overcome the horror that we went through is to confront it. I learned that you have to learn to accept it as something that happened in your life and that you can't push away the memories. They will always be there no matter how hard you try to suppress them. Dick, I know we haven't been close recently, but you can talk to me if you like. I want to be there for you. We are going to be uniquely tied to each other for the rest of our lives."

Dick knew that Karl was right. The memories from the tragedy became more and more a regular part of his every day thinking. The stress he was feeling on the tennis court allowed these memories and negative thoughts to creep into the forefront of his consciousness. Avoiding talking or thinking about the *Titanic* was just making the nightmares worse.

"Do noises ever cause you to flash back?" Dick asked. "Bleachers creaking, for instance?"

Karl nodded. "All the time."

"What do you do about that?" Dick asked, hoping for more information to sooth his soul.

"I don't think you're going to be able to avoid packed bleachers the way you're playing. I just try and focus on the good, whatever that might be at the time. It was important for me to confront and talk out my thoughts and feelings whenever I could. When I was feeling stress in other episodes of my life, say for instance in a tennis match, I could process those emotions better. Helping others and those in need also put me at ease. Being able to help my family, Helen and my child has helped me immensely. Helping you just now and having this conversation is great positive action for me."

"You are an amazing man Karl. Thank you."

"We are going to have to deal with this the rest of our lives," said Karl. "It is part of us. We just have to accept it. I'm sorry I haven't been there for you Dick. I wish I had reached out to you sooner. I wish I had done more, both while the ship was sinking and afterwards."

Did he really just hear Karl say that? Karl probably did more on the *Carpathia* to help people than anyone besides the captain. So many people, not least of which Dick, were grateful to have the assistance from Karl in those hours and days after they were rescued. Karl's alertness and awareness after the *Titanic* first hit the iceberg helped saved Helen, the Beckwiths and the Kimballs.

"Karl, you've done more to help me than anyone. I am grateful beyond words for your kindness and assistance during our days on the *Carpathia*. And look at you now! You're a husband and a father, just like you always wanted. Your dreams have come true. You were a hero to many people on that ship and now you are hero to your family. You are a blessed man. That little boy you have – and his beautiful mother, your wife – are more precious than any sterling silver trophy there is in the world of tennis."

"Thank you Dick. You are right. I know you are going to have that one day as well but before that, I have a feeling that later today you are going to add a nice piece of silver to your collection of tennis trophies. I can just feel it."

26

September 1, 1914. It was a picturesque, perfect, late-summer day in Newport, Rhode Island with just a slight breeze coming from the ocean, low humidity and just enough heat to test the fitness of America's two greatest tennis players. For the second year in a row Dick Williams of Philadelphia was challenging the great Maurice McLoughlin of San Francisco in the final of the U.S. National Championships at the Newport Casino. This was going to be the last time that the U.S. Nationals would be contested on the Casino lawns and a record crowd turned out in their finest social attire. McLoughlin had been so dominant in the tournament play the past few years that he was the heavy favorite in the match despite Dick's brilliant play in the last two rounds. What betting there was involved whether Williams would manage to win a set.

Dick felt good, though. Very good. He got a full night of sleep, had peace of mind and was ready to seize the moment. Right here, right now, this match was the most important thing in his life. He wanted this — for his father and for himself. He started a journey two and a half years ago, and even though it had been tragically derailed, he had the priceless opportunity to finish that voyage on this day.

For the first time since he arrived in the United States, he had a full personal cheering section at a tennis match. It was a revelation to Dick how comforting he found it to know there were friends in the stands rooting for him. He tried so hard to push everyone away the past two years, convincing himself that it was better that way, but he was lucky enough to find some people who stuck with him anyway. Karl and his family were there. His Uncle Norris came. His mother came for her first match ever. Even Jack Thayer took a train from Philadelphia the previous day to be there. Though of course he never looked up – he knew at every moment that there were people hanging on to every point with him.

Mac served first and held easily, as he almost always did. But at 2-2, Dick was finally able to implement Karl's advice. He stepped in on the serve on the first point, cutting off the angle and deflecting the power to the return. Mac was about knocked off of his feet. Then he did it again, and again, and broke with ease. The crowd was stunned. He held serve for 4-2 and then for 5-3 and then broke Mac again to take the first set 6-3. Two sets to go.

The second set was much tighter. Dick won the first three games in a rush, but then Mac finally picked up his level of intensity and stormed back to 3-3. From that point on, they each played the highest quality of tennis that they were capable of — and much to the crowd's delight. They held serve until it was 6-7, McLoughlin serving. The constant pressure he was putting on Mac's serve paid off again, and after getting to deuce, Dick cracked two lethal returns to break serve again and win the second set 8-6. One set away.

In previous matches, when Dick played at his highest level for over an hour, he would start to lose focus, start going for more low percentage shots and would sometimes let victory slip from his grasp. Today he was certain that it would be different. He had to stay focused because a player of the McLoughlin's caliber could easily turn a match around with this talent and shot-making. Dick stayed with his game plan

– safe and effective serving and aggressive returning. The two players went back and forth in the third set, the Newport crowd on the edge of their seats, hanging onto every stroke, gasping at every error, erupting in cheer at each winner. Mac broke Dick's serve to open the third set, offering hope for a comeback. Dick, however, immediately broke back the next game. The two then easily exchanged service holds the next eleven games.

With Mac serving at 6-7 to stay in the match, it appeared as though he would hold easily again, leading 40-15. Dick however, leaned in on two service returns, forcing volley errors to tie the score. Deuce.

After Mac lofted a forehand volley beyond the baseline, Dick stood at match point. He was just one point away from achieving his improbably victory. As quickly as visions of him holding aloft the trophy entered his mind, they were dispelled by a thunderous ace down the middle by Mac.

Deuce again.

Mac the launched consecutive bullet serves that Dick was not able to get into play. He escaped and held serve. Upset that he was not able to close out the match, Dick became slightly distracted and lost his focus, lamenting over the missed opportunity. This lack of concentration allowed Mac to break Dick's serve to take an 8-7 lead, serving to extend the match into a fourth set. He was two points away, but three errors and a winner from Dick tied the score at 8-8.

Unable to seize the opportunity, Mac's shoulders slumped. Dick was also beginning to tire, feeling the pressure of being so close to winning the title. He knew coming into the tournament that he was so fatigued from the long season that any long match would surely be the end of him, but he was so close. He could not let weariness play a factor in this match. He knew how Mac could fight and how much stamina he had as witnessed from winning the epic 17-15 set in Davis Cup against Norman Brookes.

He decided that this was the time. His moment. Hold and then break and it's over. First things first, though. Hold your serve.

He thought back to his first practice after the disaster. He closed his eyes and visualized exactly where he wanted to hit a serve. He then just shut off his brain and let his body execute.

Ace down the tee.

Flat serve out wide. Missed return.

Ace wide to the deuce court, with plenty of slice.

Flat serve down the tee. McLoughlin missed the return again.

Dick jumped to the 9-8 lead. He took a little extra time as they changed ends, savoring the moment. Everyone in the stands must have thought the set had a long way to go. No way McLoughlin would lose his serve now. But Dick knew this was it.

Remembering to get down as low as he could to return Mac's serve, he repeatedly stepped well into the court, took the ball early and on the rise, just as he had against Karl that morning. He hit three superb returns in row – two for winners, one down at Mac's feet that he couldn't handle. It was love-forty and he had three match points. Now the crowd was seeing things his way, cheering him on to win or exhorting Mac to stay alive. He didn't know which and didn't care.

The serve came hard and wide on the ad court. Two quick steps in, an abbreviated backhand stroke, catching the ball perfectly, waist-high, doing no more than redirecting the force back across the net, on a perfect trajectory down the sideline. He knew the match was over even before the ball bounced, before the crowd exploded in applause. He was the champion of the United States.

He tossed his trusty Wright & Ditson "Pim" high into the air and ran towards his friend, who was already at the net, having serve-and-volleyed as usual. They shared a hearty handshake and Mac looked him in the eye.

"You did it, Dick. Well done." The sun glinted off his freckled face. "We've played so much together. It's always been so close. It was bound to come sooner or later. Nothing I could do against you today."

"Thank you, Mac. I was lucky, I guess. I...I don't know what to say." It meant so much that the victory came against this great champion, on whom his father had been so focused, but it meant even more that he had been able to call Mac a friend.

They walked together towards the umpire to shake his hand, even as the gentleman was shouting out as loudly as he could, "Game, set, and match, Mr. Williams, six games to three, eight games to six, and ten games to eight!"

Dick looked over at his friends. His mother and uncle were hugging, tears of joy streaming down his mother's face. Jack was hugging a beautiful young girl beside him. Richard waved his top hat wildly and kissed Sallie. Karl kissed Karl, Jr., then Helen, then Karl, Jr. again. He looked at Dick and gave him a thumbs up.

Dick thought about all those hours on the practice court with his father, about all the tournaments they traveled to, about the moleskin notebooks and the McLoughlin impressions. He thought about the way his father's face brightened whenever he talked about tennis, the way even talking about tournament scheduling would send him into a frenzy of excitement, about how much he would love to be there right at this moment, in this jam-packed Newport grandstand to see his son trade blows with the greatest player in the land. He thought about his final words and about the postcard his mother showed him.

What made him happy? Being on a court in front of thousands of people playing against the best player in the country. Hitting great shots. His friends made him happy – those back at Harvard and in the stands with him today and the imposing redhead with whom he had just defeated. Seeing his mother outside of the house, truly enjoying herself — that made him happy. Trying to figure out what he was going to do with the rest of his life, discovering passions, having the freedom and confidence to do anything he wanted to do. Going to school at Harvard, representing his country in Davis Cup and reading a great book. Those things all made him happy. Life, being alive and living it to its fullest. This moment. He was happy. He was the national tennis champion of the United States.

Dick caught Karl's eye again, and mouthed "Thank you." For many reasons he wouldn't have been able to do this without Karl. Everything came rushing back into his head: the jolt on the ship, the smokestack falling like a bolt from the heavens, the numbing water, the saving ship, the pain-wracked legs, and the endless walks, up and down the deck, with a new comrade. Together, they'd made the greatest comeback in history.

Epilogue

Following his victory at the 1914 U.S. Nationals, Richard Norris Williams went on to win the singles title at the tournament that is now known as the US Open again in 1916, this time at Forest Hills, defeating William Johnston in the final. He served in the United States Army during World War I, where he received both the *Croix de Guerre* and the *Legion of Honor* for his service. After the war, Dick was able to secure a doubles title at Wimbledon, pairing with Charles Garland to win the title in 1920. He remained active with the U.S. Davis Cup team, serving as the playing-captain of the team from 1921-1926, all Cup-winning years when the team was led by the great Bill Tilden, the man who a young Dick beat en route to winning the 1912 Pennsylvania State Championships, his first tournament after the *Titanic* disaster. In 1924, he was a member of the U.S. Olympic team that competed in Paris and, despite a sprained ankle, he won the gold medal in mixed doubles with Hazel Wightman. In 1934, he returned to the Davis Cup fold as the non-playing U.S. captain, guiding the United States to the Challenge Round, where it was defeated by the Fred Perry-led team from Britain. Dick married twice, first in 1919 to Jean Haddock, and after she passed away in 1929, he married again in 1930 to Sue W. Gilmore. He had four children – Duane N. Williams, Richard N. Williams III, Quincy N. Williams and Sue Williams. In his late 1940s, he retired from competitive tennis but continued to play the game recreationally, always known as an amiable player who would hit balls with anyone, no matter what level the player. Following his love for history, he became the Director of the Historical Society of Pennsylvania for twenty years. He was inducted into the International Tennis Hall of Fame in 1957. He passed away on June 2, 1968 at the age of 77.

Karl Behr continued to stay active in tennis after the 1914 U.S. Nationals, finishing in the top ten again in 1915. Perhaps the biggest victory of his career came that year in winning the singles title in Seabright, New Jersey, defeating none other than Maurice McLoughlin 8-6, 7-5, 7-5 in the final. He was unable to serve in the war due to his German parentage, but in 1916 he was instrumental in organizing the Preparedness Parade, a demonstration that showed that the United States was ready to be involved in the war. He and Helen went on to have three more children in addition to Karl Jr. – Peter Behr, James Behr and Sally Behr. In 1925, he became the vice president of Dillon Reed, an investment bank, and continued to work in banking and finance throughout his life. He passed away on October 15, 1949 at the age of 64 and was posthumously inducted into the International Tennis Hall of Fame in 1969. After his death, Helen married Karl's friend and frequent doubles partner Dean Mathey. She passed away on September 7, 1965.

Author's Note

The true story of Dick Williams and Karl Behr and their survival from the sinking of the *Titanic* and their lives following the tragedy is remarkable. In turning it into a book of narrative form, my intention was to showcase these two amazing individuals and bring their story more to life in an appealing way that can attract a larger audience. In order to create a narrative, I had to infer thoughts and feelings and create dialogue and scenes to advance the plot. In doing so, I hope to have still honored the facts and the reality of the inspiring lives I was portraying.

On April 10, 1912, Richard Norris Williams and his father, Charles Duane Williams, were on their way to the St. Lazare train station in Paris. Fresh from a night at the Opera where they had seen *The Count of Luxembourg*, they were running late as they had gone to the wrong train station. They made their train with moments to spare and were on board the *Transatlantique* express train to the Port of Cherbourg, where they would board the *Titanic*. Richard Norris, or Dick as he was also called, was an accomplished tennis player in Switzerland and was traveling to America to play tennis and take classes at Harvard. His father Charles was a very popular man in Switzerland and had a great love for the sport of tennis. He did in fact discuss the concept of an international governing body for tennis.

On board the train, Dick did recognize Karl Behr, a top ten tennis player in America, member of the 1907 U.S. Davis Cup team who was also a Wimbledon doubles finalist in 1907. Dick had not met him as of yet, but did recognize him. Karl was on the train on the way to meet the love of his life, Helen Newsom. Karl had traveled to Europe in pursuit of Helen, masking it as a business trip. He had journeyed around Europe for ten days with Helen and her disapproving mother Sallie and their family before separating in Nice to go and conduct business in Vienna. A few days before the *Titanic* set sail, he received a telegram from Helen saying she was going to set sail on the famed ship and asking him to join her.

There were few detailed accounts of the days on the *Titanic* and certain scenes were created to try and illustrate life on the ship, such as the dining and smoke room scenes and the squash match (although there was indeed a squash court on the ship.) It is known that Dick and Charles spent time with John and Jack Thayer, Major Archibald Butt and Frances Millet, the Wideners and William Dulles. They spent time in the gym (with the friendly gym attendant Thomas McCawley) and in the smoking room. They loved to walk the decks of the ship. These are all real people and real back stories – John Thayer was a star cricket player turned railway tycoon. Major Archibald Butt was indeed President Roosevelt's and President Taft's main military aide and his good friend Frances Millet was a famous painter. The Millet-Butt Memorial Fountain in Washington, D.C. was erected in their honor after the disaster. The Wideners were one of the richest families in Pennsylvania and Harry Widener was indeed a Bibelot. The Harry Elkins Widener Memorial Library still exists today on the Harvard campus. The White Star employee Miss Newton was, however, made up.

Karl, meanwhile, spent his time on the ship frolicking with Helen whenever he got a chance and trying to win the approval of Sallie Beckwith. Richard Beckwith, the Kimballs, the Warrens and the Chibnalls are all real people, though little is known about their personalities and back stories, although Edwin Kimball was the president of a piano company and the Chibnalls were active in the women's rights movement.

The actual conversations and scenes on board the ship are imagined. There is no record of what these people were actually saying to one another, the exact ways they spent their days, or the thoughts that were going through their heads prior to the evening the ship hit an iceberg on April 14, 1912. However, I based it all on extensive research and with the intention of bringing incredible true stories and true people to life.

However, there were very detailed accounts available about the night of the sinking. Dick and Charles spent the evening at the Captain's Dinner held by the Wideners. After the dinner in the smoke room, Charles told the story about the *Arizona* and how he and his shipmates used cotton to plug the hole caused by the iceberg. That night the Williams felt a jolt from the iceberg while they were sleeping. When they left their room to investigate, Dick did indeed help free a passenger who was trapped in her room and was threatened to be reported by a stewardess. They went to the deck of the ship, went to get their life-vests, saw the procession of bread and mail coming from the lower decks, went to the smoke room and went to the gym. They remained calm throughout the night. As the ship was going down, a gigantic steam pipe fell on Charles, killing him, while Dick was able to swim to a collapsed lifeboat, where he hung on throughout the night. The accounts and details of his survival through the night are also true.

Karl, meanwhile, ran to check on Helen the moment he felt the impact of the iceberg. They went to check the upper decks, and although everything was calm and empty, they were alarmed when other members of their party reported seeing water on the squash courts. They went to the deck by the lifeboats and were one able to get onto the second lifeboat. When the women boarded and the lifeboat was not even half full, Mrs. Beckwith asked Bruce Ismay, the president of White Star Line, if the men could join them. He replied in exact words, "Of course, Madam, every one of you." Karl, Helen, the Beckwiths, the Kimballs, Mrs. Warren, Dr. Henry Frauenthal and Mrs. Stengel were all on board Lifeboat 5, which was the second boat launched from the *Titanic* and the second boat rescued by the *Carpathia*.

Little is known about the time on the *Carpathia*. It is known that when Dick got on board the ship, he had a sip of brandy, ate breakfast and then took a nap. When he woke up the pain in his legs was so intense that he tried to find help. The doctors on the *Carpathia* were all busy, so a passenger who was also a doctor helped him out. This doctor suggested that his legs be amputated. The alternative was that he had to walk through the pain. Karl, meanwhile, became very involved during his time on the *Carpathia* with helping others, raising funds for the third class, and forming a survivor's committee.

It is known that Dick and Karl met on April 15 on board the *Carpathia* and struck up a friendship, bonding over tennis and their time in Switzerland. The exact details of their meeting and the conversations they are not clear and are not factually documented, but Karl is described as being helpful to Dick. Creative license was taken in this book to tell this particular portion of the story and creating a scenario where Karl and Dick did officially meet.

Even less facts are known about Karl and Dick's lives after the disaster. The media was not as widespread or intrusive as it is today and most *Titanic* survivors just wanted to move on from the tragedy in any way they could. We do know that after the *Carpathia* docked in New York, Dick went to live with his uncle in Chestnut Hill, Pennsylvania and enrolled in Harvard in the fall. His mother came over from Switzerland to live in Boston. Karl, meanwhile, did in fact testify in the *Titanic* hearings at the Waldorf Astoria and did endure newspaper headlines reporting his romance with Helen on board the ship. He took some time away from tennis and became officially engaged to Helen at the Behr lake house. The details of their wedding are just as they were reported in the media. Karl did struggle with survivor's guilt.

All of the tennis tournaments and scores are factual. Dick did indeed win a tournament a mere six weeks after his legs were threatened to be amputated. His first loss on American soil was to Karl Behr at Longwood tournament just outside of Boston. Dick formed a friendly rivalry with his Davis Cup teammate Maurice McLoughlin (they indeed went travelling together around Europe and stumbled upon a tennis tournament in the mountains of France, where Dick was recognized and remembered fondly). Karl, meanwhile, kept coming back to tennis in between marrying Helen and starting a family.

In 1914 at the U.S. Nationals – the tournament that is now the US Open – Karl and Dick met each other in the quarterfinals. Dick won the match of *Titanic* survivors easily and went on to finally win the singles title, defeating McLoughlin in the final in a match called by the *New York Times* as "one of the great upsets of the age." It was the last U.S. Nationals match played at The Casino in Newport, Rhode Island, now the home of the International Tennis Hall of Fame.

-Lindsay Gibbs
Brooklyn, New York
January, 2012

Acknowledgements

There are so many people to thank for helping this book come to life that I don't know where to start, so I suppose I'll start at the beginning. To Randy Walker, the Managing Partner for New Chapter Press, the publisher of this book, thank you for discovering these stories and coming up with the idea for making it into a book. Thank you for (some unknown reason) entrusting the story with me.

To the families of Karl Behr and Richard Norris Williams, especially Quincy Williams and Django Haskins, thank you for the information you provided and for sharing your stories, writings and family history.

I could not have made it through this project without my family. Thanks to my mom, Bo Berry Gibbs, for her unyielding belief in me and for providing refuge when I needed to escape from New York City to write. To my Dad and Stepmom, Allen and Carlene Gibbs, thank you for your unconditional support and for never questioning me when I told you I was quitting my day job to write a novel. To my amazing extended family on the Gibbs and Berry sides – Granny, Grandad, Munya, and all my Aunts, Uncles, Cousins and Stepbrothers – it would take another novel to thank you all individually, but I am forever indebted to you all for your love and support.

This book would have been nothing without a whole lot of research and for that I needed a lot of assistance. I was especially aided by the books *A Night to Remember* by Walter Lord, *Titanic: An Illustrated History* by Donald Lynch, *Ti-*

tanic: Destination Disaster" by John P. Eaton and Charles A. Haas, *Covering the Court* by Al Laney and *For The Love of The Game* by Maurice McLoughlin. In addition, the *Encyclopedia Titanica*, the *New York Times* historical archives, the *Titanic Inquiry Project* and *The Art of Lawn and Tennis Guides* from 1907-1914 were instrumental in weaving together the facts that were the backbone of this novel. *The Bud Collins History of Tennis* was also an excellent resource for research.

Helen Behr Stanford, the granddaughter of Karl Behr, recently released a novel *Starboard at Midnight*, chronicling the life of Karl (and Helen) in great detail. That book was an excellent resource as we tried to fill in the holes and make the story as factual as possible.

The International Tennis Hall of Fame in Newport, Rhode Island was immensely helpful for me in gathering information. I particularly have to thank Nicole Markham and Troy Gowen, who were very hospitable to me in May of 2011 when I visited. I also want to thank Marshall Jon Fisher, the author of the fantastic tennis book *A Terrible Splendor* and the upcoming tennis novel *A Backhanded Gift* for his help and assistance.

And lastly, thank you to my many friends and loved ones who provided encouraging words when I needed them the most, especially Margie and Jay Motsinger, Nancy Prairie, Carly Bendzans, Marianna Jackson, Michelle Coughlan, Amanda Hogan, Erin Gilmore, George Robert Morse, Andy Pidcock, Annie Sumberg, Kay Maddox and Meredith Skeeters. Thanks for dealing with me during my melt-downs, believing in me when I didn't believe in myself, and still being my friend after I fell off the face of the earth for six months.

Also From New Chapter Press

The Education of a Tennis Player
—BY ROD LAVER AND BUD COLLINS

Rod Laver's first-hand account of his historic 1969 Grand Slam sweep of all four major tennis titles is documented in this memoir, written by Laver along with co-author and tennis personality Bud Collins. The book details his childhood, early career and his most important matches. The four-time Wimbledon champion and the only player in tennis history to win two Grand Slams also sprinkles in tips and lessons on how players of all levels can improve their games. Originally published in 1971, *The Education of a Tennis Player* was updated in 2009 on the 40th anniversary of his historic second Grand Slam with new content, including the story of his recovery from a near-fatal stroke in 1998.

The Bud Collins History of Tennis—BY BUD COLLINS

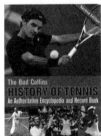

Compiled by the most famous tennis journalist and historian in the world, this book is the ultimate compilation of historical tennis information, including year-by-year recaps of every tennis season, biographical sketches of every major tennis personality, as well as stats, records, and championship rolls for all the major events. The author's personal relationships with major tennis stars offer insights into the world of professional tennis found nowhere else.

The Wimbledon Final That Never Was...—BY SIDNEY WOOD

A fascinating compilation of tennis stories and observations collected over nearly a century, Wimbledon champion Sidney Wood's memoir is a must for tennis acionados. The signature story is Wood winning the 1931 Wimbledon title over Frank Shields — his school buddy, doubles partner, roommate, Davis Cup teammate and grandfather of Brooke Shields — in one of the most curious episodes in sports history.